At David C Cook, we equip the local church around the corner and around the globe to make disciples. Come see how we are working together—go to **www.davidccook.org**. Thank you!

transforming lives together

What people are saying about …

RANKIN WILBOURNE
AND
UNION WITH CHRIST

"Everyone seems to agree that union with Christ is a biblical teaching crucial to understanding and communicating the gospel, but preachers today do not give it the same emphasis that the New Testament does. One reason is that, unlike the new birth, justification, and adoption, it requires multiple metaphors to draw out its rich meaning. Rankin does so clearly and compellingly. This is simply the best book for laypeople on this subject. It is grounded in exegesis and theology and yet is lucid and supremely practical. While not unaware of the recent controversies about union and justification, which are briefly sketched in the endnotes, Rankin's whole concern is to make the biblical teaching accessible and applicable to the reader. He does this with excellence."

—**Tim Keller**, senior pastor of Redeemer
Presbyterian Church, New York City

"I'm trying to remember the last time I was more excited about a new book or a new author. Rankin Wilbourne brings a remarkable flair for writing, a great breadth and depth of learning, and a passionate heart to the most important subject in the world: What is the true and sufficient destiny for human life? … Rankin does a masterful job of articulating what union with Christ consists of, how central it is to the writers of Scripture and to great thinkers through the centuries, why it has been lost in our day, and most importantly how to pursue it as a concrete reality in daily life for ordinary people. So that's why I'm excited for you to meet Rankin and enter a new world."

—**John Ortberg**, senior pastor of Menlo Church; author of *I'd Like You More if You Were More Like Me* and *Eternity Is Now in Session*

"Before 2016, we had no readable survey of union with Christ for lay readers—a book that is theologically robust, but not too heavy, well-illustrated, and also well-applied to the demands of everyday life. That's because such an approachable feat is nearly impossible. Wilbourne pulled it off. What I find most impressive about this book is the balance between celebrating the truth of our union and calling us to feed off this glorious reality in our labors toward holiness."

—**Tony Reinke**, naming *Union with Christ* one of Desiring God's top books of 2016

"Highly recommended for all readers. Offers biblical, historical, and practical perspective on this most vital doctrine."

—**Collin Hansen**, editorial director of The Gospel Coalition

THE
CROSS
BEFORE ME

THE
CROSS
BEFORE ME

RANKIN
WILBOURNE

BRIAN
GREGOR

REIMAGINING
THE WAY TO THE
GOOD LIFE

DAVID C COOK

transforming lives together

THE CROSS BEFORE ME
Published by David C Cook
4050 Lee Vance Drive
Colorado Springs, CO 80918 U.S.A.

Integrity Music Limited, a Division of David C Cook
Brighton, East Sussex BN1 2RE, England

The graphic circle C logo is a registered trademark of David C Cook.

The website addresses recommended throughout this book are offered as a
resource to you. These websites are not intended in any way to be or imply an
endorsement on the part of David C Cook, nor do we vouch for their content.

Library of Congress Control Number 2019939640
ISBN 978-0-7814-1333-6
eISBN 978-0-8307-7859-1

The Team: Alice Crider, Jeff Gerke, Rachael Stevenson,
Kayla Fenstermaker, Susan Murdock
Cover Design: James Hershberger

Printed in the United States of America
First Edition 2019

1 2 3 4 5 6 7 8 9 10

062819

To my children,
May you grow to see that this is the
way to the life that is truly life.
R. W.

To Thomas and Esmé,
In love and joy.
B. G.

For whoever wants to save their life will lose it,
but whoever loses their life for me will find it.

Matthew 16:25 NIV

I'm just sick of ego, ego, ego. My own and everybody else's.
I'm sick of everybody that wants to get somewhere, do something
distinguished and all, be somebody interesting. It's disgusting.

J. D. Salinger, *Franny and Zooey*

If I had a message to my contemporaries it is surely this: Be anything
you like, be madmen, drunks, and bastards of every shape and form,
but at all costs avoid one thing: success.... If you are too obsessed with
success, you will forget to live. If you have learned only how to be a
success, your life has probably been wasted.

Thomas Merton, *Love and Living*

CONTENTS

INTRODUCTION

Twelve hundred Yale University students—nearly *one quarter* of the entire undergraduate body—enrolled in a 2018 course on happiness entitled Psychology and the Good Life, taught by Dr. Laurie Santos. It was the most popular course in the history of the school, so popular it was only offered once, as its massive enrollment affected so many other classes. A similar course at Harvard in 2006 had drawn nine hundred students and was touted as the most popular course in the history of that university. Why would so many of the most gifted students in America flock to courses on personal happiness?

"The fact that a class like this has such large interest," one of Dr. Santos's students speculated, "speaks to how tired students are of numbing their emotions—both positive and negative—so they can focus on their work, the next step, the next accomplishment." Perhaps these students had thought that getting into the university of their dreams would make them happy. They must have made many sacrifices to get where they were. But they found themselves still feeling anxious, not yet happy, and they didn't know where they went wrong.

Dr. Santos says that her students were not alone in feeling this way. "Scientists didn't realize this in the same way [ten] or so years ago, that our intuitions about what will make us happy, like winning the lottery and getting a good grade—are totally wrong."[1]

If our intuitions are totally wrong, how can we learn what we should pursue? How can we know what will make us happy? It's an important question because while we may not know what will bring us the happiness we seek, we do know that what we're trying isn't working. And it's not just highly motivated college students who are experiencing this frustration.

FRUSTRATED AMBITION

Andre Agassi hated tennis. One of the most decorated American tennis players, eight-time Grand Slam winner, Agassi went from the long-haired rebel people loved to hate to the shaved-head champion people loved to root for. Yet Agassi has now confided that through it all he hated tennis, even at his moments of greatest personal triumph.[2] He wrote in his autobiography, *Open*, "Now that I've won a slam, I know something that very few people on earth are permitted to know. A win doesn't feel as good as a loss feels bad, and the good feeling doesn't last as long as the bad. Not even close."[3]

If he didn't enjoy tennis, why did he keep playing it, hour upon hour, day after day, week after week, month after month? Couldn't the same question be asked of many of us: Why do we keep doing what we know isn't working?

Andre Agassi is certainly not the first athlete or celebrity to experience the profound disappointment that comes with smashing success, worldwide acclaim, and inconceivable wealth. Millions watched Tom Brady's interview on *60 Minutes* after his third Super Bowl victory. (He now has six rings and counting and is widely considered the GOAT—greatest of all time—in professional football.) Toward the end of that interview, Brady said, "Why do I have three Super Bowl rings and still think there's something greater out there for me? I mean, maybe a lot of people would say, 'Hey man, this is what is.' I reached my goal, my dream, my life. Me, I think, 'God, it's got to be more than this.' I mean this isn't, this can't be what it's all cracked up to be."

The interviewer interrupted the ensuing silence with a question: "What's the answer?" Brady responded, "I wish I knew," and then repeated, "I wish I knew."[4]

Tom Brady and Andre Agassi both speak from the absolute pinnacle of their professions, unfamiliar heights for almost all of us. Yet they express a feeling familiar to many of us. We all want to be happy, but we don't know what will make us happy. The twentieth-century writer Thomas Merton captures this tension precisely: "Why do we have to spend our lives striving to be something that we would never want to be, if we only knew what we wanted? Why do we waste our time doing things which, if we only stopped to think about them, are just the opposite of what we were made for?"[5]

But that's just it: *if only* we knew what we wanted! We are like arrows ceaselessly seeking a target. Yet the search for happiness is irrepressible. The seventeenth-century philosopher and mathematician

Blaise Pascal writes, "All men seek happiness. This is without exception. Whatever different means they employ, they all tend to this end. The cause of some going to war, and of others avoiding it, is the same desire in both, attended with different views. The will never takes the least step but to this object. This is the motive of every action of every man, even of those who hang themselves."[6]

Place Merton alongside Pascal, and the tension is set. It is agonizing—and not just for celebrities and sports stars and hyperdriven college kids. We all want to be happy. The "pursuit of Happiness" is enshrined as an unalienable right in the Declaration of Independence. We spend our days seeking happiness, but we don't know how to get it, and our intuitions about how to find it are almost entirely wrong. What are we to do?

This tension is not abstract, although we may not be able to put our finger on it. We feel our longing to be happy so deeply, which is why we keep moving—jumping from book to book, turning from juice cleanse to fad diet, clicking from show to show, scrolling from post to post. We are searching for a happiness that will finally bring us some rest.

As the pace of our collective search has become more frantic, there's been an explosion of books on happiness and human flourishing in recent years, from international bestsellers to business books, highbrow to popular, Christian books to psychology and self-help, even the backlash "rebellion" books *against* happiness.[7] This trend is not only on bookshelves but can be found in scientific circles as well, with the surging popularity of positive psychology, which the scientific study of human flourishing and what science can teach us about what makes for a healthier and happier life.[8] From *The Happiness Project* to *The Happiness Hypothesis* to chart-topping songs, happiness is *in*.

WHY DO WE NEED ANOTHER BOOK ON HAPPINESS?

With all these books on the topic, past and present, why add one more to an already-overcrowded bookshelf? Do we really need another book on happiness? As a pastor and a philosopher, we think we do because, though everyone seems to be talking about happiness, there's something almost no one seems to be saying. Let's get at it by way of a story.

Unbroken by Laura Hillenbrand was an international bestseller that turned into a major motion picture. The book tells the story of Louis Zamperini, an Olympic track star whose athletic career was interrupted by World War II. For the first half of his life, Zamperini's resilience and grit helped him survive a series of horrific ordeals.

He survived a plane crash in the Pacific theater of the war. He spent forty-seven days drifting on a life raft, catching rainwater as he could, trying to fish as he was able. On that raft, he was shot at by enemy aircraft and circled by ravenous sharks. He was finally rescued, but alas, by the Japanese. He spent more than two and a half years as a prisoner of war, was tortured, physically and mentally, by his captors, the most menacing of whom was known as the Bird. He was stretched far beyond his ability to endure, but somehow he survived. He was finally rescued and returned home.

This riveting tale of one man's resilience has inspired millions. The book was so popular that many missed the irony of its title, *Unbroken*. It's true that Zamperini had incredible determination and an almost indomitable will to never give up.

But the book doesn't end with Zamperini being liberated from his prison camp and going home. He comes home and gets married, and the same grit and resolve that enabled him to survive the prison camp take a dark turn. His marriage suffers horribly, and he's mostly to blame. He becomes an alcoholic. He cannot let go of the deep anger he feels toward his captors, the Bird in particular. He dreams of returning to Japan to seek his vengeance. He cannot forgive those who mistreated him. Though he is free in America, in many ways he remains imprisoned.

Zamperini had thought his life was saved when he was finally liberated from that prison camp. But that was not when he became free. That was not his moment of redemption. Not until his indomitable spirit is finally *broken* is he set free from his anger and resentment, set free from his pain, set free to live in a way he never had before.

Unbroken may be the book's title, but Hillenbrand makes clear through the structure of her book that Zamperini's life is not saved until he is broken. A plane crash couldn't do it, forty-seven days adrift at sea couldn't do it, not even two and a half years in a prison camp could break him. Not until his marriage is failing and he finds himself lost in a bottle, unable to make his own life work, does he have an experience with God. Zamperini's life turns when he is touched by God at a Billy Graham crusade in a tent in downtown Los Angeles. It is only when he is broken that Louis Zamperini breaks through to a new life.[9]

Our book is written in the conviction that while Zamperini's story is extraordinary, anyone who wants to find the life that is truly life must follow in that same way, the broken way, though it will take different forms for each of us. No other way but losing our lives will bring us the rest and happiness we long for in this life.

That's why we set Zamperini's story alongside two of the most accomplished athletes of recent memory, fierce competitors with an insatiable need to win. Because they, from the top of their respective mountains, are telling us that climbing the mountain of personal accomplishment does not work, it is not the way to happiness. What is the way? That's what this book is about. We need this additional book on happiness because even though everyone seems to be talking about it, here's what almost no one seems to be saying: *Happiness is communion with God. And the way to that communion is the way of the cross.*

Our thesis is that simple and that subversive. It's ancient. It's biblical. It has a rich historical heritage. But this theme has almost disappeared—from our literature, our language, our shared understanding, and even from our churches. If the first half of our thesis is unheralded, then the second half is almost unheard of.[10]

What does a fully human, flourishing life look like? We think there is a distinctly Christian answer to this question, hard as it may be to hear on an average Sunday. The answer is not bigger, newer, shinier, or stronger. Jesus Christ grounds what makes for human flourishing in his life, death, and resurrection. Jesus shows us the distinctly Christian way to the full and free life: the cruciform way.

THE CRUCIFORM LIFE

Cruciform is a word borrowed from the world of architecture, where it describes a building laid out in the shape of a cross. Old cathedrals in particular were designed in this way, having a long sanctuary with wings near the front so that the building's footprint is cross shaped. *Cruciform* simply means "cross shaped."

The cruciform way is the cross-shaped way. And the cruciform way is God's way to the good and beautiful life he intends for us.

This seems strange to us. *Are you telling me the way to wholeness and flourishing is through loss and deprivation, through suffering and death? That seems counterproductive and counterintuitive.*

Exactly. We believe the cross has something to teach us, all of us, about what it means to live a fully human life here and now. The cross is God's wisdom for human flourishing. Not only is the cross the instrument of our salvation; it also sets a pattern for the whole art of living. The cross is more than an *ethic*, a way of doing things; it sets up a whole new way of being, fueled by a whole new way of seeing. Everything must now be interpreted in light of the cross.[11]

Our book revolves around one question: What does the cross—the most iconic religious symbol in the world—have to teach us about the way to happiness and the good and beautiful life?

More simply: What does the cross have to teach us about the art of living?

We might as well get out of the way that being called to a cross-shaped life doesn't sound either good or beautiful. That sort of life sounds like suffering, pain, and humiliation. It sounds like death. It sounds like something to run *from*, not something to move toward. It sounds like the opposite of what would lead to our peace and joy. Yes. We understand.

But "the word of the cross" (1 Cor. 1:18) has always been a stumbling block. In the ancient world, the cross of Christ was a scandal to Roman, Greek, and Jewish minds. It was foolishness to believe that almighty God would reveal himself in such a humble and humiliating fashion. Part of our burden in this project is to recover this scandal for an audience that has domesticated the cross or reduced it to merely the private place where Jesus died for your personal sins.

THE CROSS BEFORE ME

In many ways this whole book is an extended reflection on one line from Jesus, "Whoever finds his life will lose it, and whoever loses his life for my sake will find it" (Matt. 10:39; see also Mark 8:35; Luke 9:24).

This idea is one of the most enigmatic things Jesus ever expressed. And precisely because it is so compact (and so contrary to our experience), we tend to read over it as just another one of those paradoxes we sometimes hear: the way up is down; die that we may truly live; blessed are the poor. They are so counterintuitive but familiar that they've almost become clichés. *Yes, Jesus was always saying paradoxical things like that.* Perhaps we package it (away?) as a paradox so we don't have to experience it.

We may say these phrases with our mouths, but we can't seem to embrace them experientially with our hearts and lives. *You mean really? Losing my life is the way to find life?* Do we in fact believe that Jesus was telling us the truth—the way things actually work in the universe we are living in? If we believed what Jesus said so plainly, wouldn't it change what we were afraid of and anxious about and ambitious for?

On the tombstone of the Russian novelist Fyodor Dostoyevsky is the verse he chose as the epigraph for his final novel, *The Brothers Karamazov.* Dostoyevsky converted to Christianity as an adult when someone slipped him a copy of the New Testament while he was in prison. His novels are filled with existential and theological questions. He's one of the greatest writers of world literature who grappled with the deepest questions of human existence in thousands of pages and millions of words. What would he pick, then, as the epigraph of his final book? Here was the verse he selected: "Truly, truly, I say to you, unless a grain of wheat falls into the earth and dies, it remains alone; but if it dies, it bears much fruit" (John 12:24).

Those are words Jesus spoke to his disciples. And in the next verse he told them, "Whoever loves his life loses it, and whoever hates his life in this world will keep it for eternal life" (v. 25).

This book is dedicated to exploring what Jesus means by this image of the grain of wheat. What must fall and die? What must be cracked open to bring new life? And how could the One who came to give us life abundant also call us to "hate" our life in this world? *What does this mean, Jesus?*

What might it look like for us today to lose our lives so as to save them? What does "losing your life" look like for ambitious, driven modern people? How can this call to downward mobility be heard as good news in an upwardly mobile world?

REIMAGINING THE WAY TO THE GOOD LIFE

We threaded stories through each chapter of this book, narratives that capture the central claim of that chapter, because we believe stories are the way humans learn best. A good story is often more effective than a tight argument. We want you to see that this cruciform way is not simply an interesting idea or a counterintuitive phrase—but rather a whole new way of being in the world, one that can reorder our desires and alter our perceptions. In order for deep change to occur in us, we don't need just our ideas to be challenged or our minds changed. Rather our wants and desires must be refined, even made new. And these can be reached only through our imaginations, the eyes of our hearts.

We don't want readers just to learn—though we hope for that as well. We want you to *reimagine* what makes for a good life, what counts as a successful life and a life worth living. Everything must now be reinterpreted in light of the cross.

What does a life worth living look like ... in light of the cross?

What sort of life should we aspire toward … in light of the cross?

What should you value for yourself and those you love … in light of the cross?

What does freedom mean … in light of the cross?

As a reader, you might have to work harder with a story—no one spells out the moral for you—but the rewards (and therefore the transformation) are exponentially greater. Through this reimagining, we want you to taste and see that the cruciform way truly is a better way to live.

A PASTOR AND A PHILOSOPHER

A final word on how the two of us came to write this book together. This book is a collaboration between two authors: one a Christian pastor, the other a Christian philosopher. In some ways, we have very different vocations, yet they have one vital thing in common: each is concerned with the care of the soul.

As Christians we believe the happiness each soul longs for is found in communion with God. That is what we were created for—to know God and find our delight in him. And as Christians we believe the path to knowing God must always go by way of the cross. Historically the notion that all knowledge of God must be interpreted in light of the cross has been called the *theology of the cross*.

For both of us the theology of the cross has been a long-standing interest. For Rankin it began almost two decades ago when he read a commentary on a classic sixteenth-century text by Martin Luther, where Luther contrasts *theologians of glory* with *theologians of the cross* (and according to Luther, we are all theologians, in that we all have ideas about ultimate things). Thus, the phrase *theology of the cross* is often attributed to Luther.[12]

But Luther, who famously says, "The cross alone is our theology,"[13] would have been the first to insist that this insight was not his own. In many ways, it's the core of Paul's message to the church in Corinth. You can find this theme stitched throughout Paul's letters and indeed throughout the New Testament.[14] Paul claimed in one of his most famous passages that this theme did not emerge from him but comes from God's own self-revelation in Christ: "God chose the foolish things of the world to shame the wise; God chose the weak things of the world to shame the strong. God chose the lowly things of this world and the despised things—and the things that are not—to nullify the things that are, so that no one may boast before him" (1 Cor. 1:27–29 NIV).

God deliberately chose to turn our normal expectations of wisdom and strength upside down—to nullify them—so that no one might boast before him. Rankin, a former banker and a naturally competitive person, became fascinated with the question of what this means for the shape of our lives today, for our vocations and ambitions. *What does a theology of the cross look like in daily living? What does this mean for my job? Am I supposed to be mediocre now? Should I not try to win anymore?*

These questions seized his imagination as potentially life altering, but he found few books that addressed his questions adequately and for the layperson.[15] More distressing, as a pastor he wondered whether we who claim to know Christ actually *believe* that Jesus' cruciform way is the way to the full and free life. He wondered whether *he* even believed this. If so, why was he so afraid of failure? What if contentment comes by way of subtraction and not addition?[16]

For Brian the theology of the cross has been a central theme in his philosophical work. It began in grad school, when he noticed the way Luther's theology of the cross influenced major philosophers like Hegel and Heidegger. What Brian found perplexing was that as these philosophers translated the cross into philosophical categories, they lost the real scandal of the cross. Brian's question became, What would a truly cruciform philosophy look like? Or more simply, What does the cross of Jesus teach us about what it means to be fully human? This became the central question of his dissertation and first book, *A Philosophical Anthropology of the Cross: The Cruciform Self.*[17]

We met in early 2014, shortly after Brian and his family moved to Los Angeles for a teaching position. Actually, our wives were the first to meet, and they bonded over shared literary interests. Great wives that they are, they put us in touch with each other. And when we discovered our shared theological interests, we thought, *We should write a book together!*

This is that book. Our goal here is to make the theology of the cross accessible and practicable for a broad audience. A more robust vision of spiritual formation that captures our imaginations is simply not possible without a thorough understanding of what life under the cross looks like beyond the pew, day to day. If we want happiness, if we desire the abundant life Jesus promised, we must get there his way—the way of the cross must become our way of life. This book aims to show what a cruciform life looks like.

THE SHAPE OF THIS BOOK

Chapters 1 and 2 lay out our basic argument. Chapter 1 spells out our big idea in detail. Chapter 2, "The Scandal of the Cross: Then and Now," amplifies the claim that the cross of Christ as the wisdom of God has always been *beyond* counterintuitive. It is subversive and scandalous, and it will appear as folly. The cross was offensive to ancient sensibilities and their conception of the good life. We need to recover a fresh sense of that scandal today.

Chapter 3 gets right into what may be your immediate question: How does this vision of human flourishing upend and reshape how we do what we do and why we do it? How does the cross re-form our ambitions and our work?

Chapter 4 examines what a life that pursues the grace of humility looks like. Chapter 5 shows how this vision of human flourishing redefines a buzzword of our current cultural moment: *freedom*. Freedom in the cruciform life is freedom from self-justification, which makes us free for communion with God and others.

Chapter 6 looks at one of today's leading contenders for what we think we need in order to be fulfilled—deeply satisfying romantic love—and shows how the cruciform life transforms this desire and reshapes our understanding of love. Chapter 7 shows how pain and suffering, while undesirable and never to be sought in and of themselves, are necessary for knowing God.

Chapter 8 takes up a question looming over this entire project: If our ultimate hope lies in the next life, where there will be no more tears, then is the call to take up our cross simply a call to grin and bear it? No! In this world the cruciform life really is your best life now. Knowing that the end is joy is what makes joy and peace possible even along the hard and narrow way (Ps. 84:5–7; 126:4–6; Matt. 7:14).

Chapter 9 demonstrates how to weave this high and demanding call into our daily habits and practices. How do you weave this pursuit into the pattern of your daily life? For followers of Jesus, the pursuit of happiness turns out to be the pursuit of godliness, in solitude and in community, and this pursuit has to become habituated through learning to delight in the cruciform way. The re-forming of our desires will take training many of us are unaccustomed to.

This book is dedicated to all those students of Dr. Santos who heard "Our intuitions about what will make us happy … are totally wrong," but who don't know how to replace those intuitions. It is to all those courageously admitting, "I wish I knew," or lamenting, "It's got to be more than this."

Our culture is having a wisdom contest about what makes for a fully human life and how we can be happy. This book offers an unheralded option, a minority report: the cruciform path is God's wisdom for human flourishing.

1

THE CROSS AND THE ART OF HUMAN FLOURISHING

We all live with the objective of being happy, our lives are all different and yet the same.

Anne Frank, *Diary of a Young Girl*

All men seek happiness. This is without exception. Whatever different means they employ, they all tend to this end.

Blaise Pascal, *Pensées*

We all want to be happy, but we don't know what will make us happy, and our intuitions about what will lead to our happiness are often entirely wrong. This book asks a strange question: What does the cross have to teach us about happiness and the art of living the good and beautiful life?

In the ancient world the cross was an instrument of torture—of suffering, humiliation, and death. It was not venerated; it was feared. No one wanted to commemorate it, much less wear it as a symbol around one's neck. It was too painful, too shameful.

Death by crucifixion was so agonizing that a new word was coined to describe it: *excruciating*. The sight of crosses lining the Roman roads leading into the capital city would have evoked dread and terror in the imaginations of first-century men and women.[1]

Today the cross is the most iconic religious symbol in the world, revered by Christians as the instrument of human salvation and celebrated as the place where Jesus died to take away the sin of the world. It decorates hills and homes, biceps and necklines.

But what if the cross is more than we realize? What if the cross is not just a memorial of the world's most important event but also a revelation of God's wisdom for this world here and now? What if the cross is a perpetual challenge to our notions of glory and greatness and an ongoing indictment of our most ingrained ways of thinking and valuing? What if God's way for a human life to flourish is the cruciform way?

AN INTRODUCTION TO THE CRUCIFORM LIFE

Cruciform, we said in the introduction, is a word taken from the context of architecture. Many older cathedrals and church buildings were designed in such a way that their footprint made the shape of a cross with an extended sanctuary flanked by wings near the front for additional seating. *Cruciform* simply means in the shape of a cross.

The thesis of this book is that God's way to human flourishing is the cruciform way. The good and beautiful life is the cruciform life, a life not only saved by but also shaped by the cross. This is the unique and unheralded path to the life we have always wanted. It is the way to what Jesus calls the blessed life (Matt. 5:3) and what Paul calls "the life that is truly life" (1 Tim. 6:19 NIV). The cross of Jesus has something to teach everyone created in God's image, which is every one of us, about the art of living as our Maker intended us to live.

That might sound intriguing, even oddly beautiful. But most of us don't believe it, not really. If we did, instead of dreading what disappointed us, we'd embrace unmet expectations as moving us further along. "Thank you," we would say to anything that humbled us. Failure would become a friend, and our egos would become our enemies. The cross is God's *strange* way. It shows us we have to lose the life we've always thought we needed in order to find the life we've always wanted.

This theme of the cruciform life is ancient and biblical, but for the most part it has disappeared from our literature and language today, even from our churches. This is not surprising in a culture that cherishes self-expression and promotes radical individualism, that prizes comfort and safety and health (and for which these are more accessible than at any other time in history). The scandal of the cross today is that it has ceased to be a scandal.

Yet the vision of the cruciform life has historically captured the imaginations of some of our best artists. It's the story line of one of the world's greatest poems, *The Divine Comedy* by Dante Alighieri. And it inspired the book that for a thousand years was second only to the Bible as the most read book in the world: *The Consolation of Philosophy*. (It had quite a run at the top of the charts, but it doesn't sound as if it would be a bestseller today, does it?) It was written by the most famous man of the sixth century: Boethius (Bo-EE-thee-us). Here's his story.[2]

HOW BOETHIUS CAN SAVE YOUR LIFE

Boethius was born into a noble family, but both of his parents died when he was young. He was adopted into another family of prestige, wealth, and influence. He became an accomplished scholar. It is because of his translations that we have some of Aristotle's works still with us today. Then he became a celebrated statesman, widely respected for his political savvy. And he married well—his wife was universally admired for her character and pedigree.

He received the highest honors of the state. Boethius was named magister officiorum, kind of like prime minister. He had two sons, and he saw them grow into honorable men and achieve some measure of his own success. These two brothers were named joint consuls at a young age. Their proud father gave the speech that day.

Are you getting the picture? Whatever you're good at, Boethius was better. Whatever you've achieved, he did more. He was the most accomplished man of his time—musician, poet, politician, scholar, orator. Here is a man who seemingly had it all. He was successful in every way possible. We don't even have a category for this kind of success today. It would be like Michael Jordan winning the Nobel Prize in Literature *and* a Congressional Medal of Honor *and* then becoming a beloved president, complete with a family everyone admired. Boethius is the original *most interesting man in the world.*

Yet less than a year after presiding over his sons' public inauguration, Boethius found himself in a solitary jail cell 350 miles from home. He had been the victim of an unjust smear campaign by his understandably envious rivals. He was falsely accused and then stripped of his honor, wealth, and friends. He was sentenced to death. Maybe this does have the makings of a bestseller after all. Except the plot doesn't turn the way we'd expect.

His book *The Consolation of Philosophy* opens with Boethius in prison. He is distraught, indignant over the injustice of it all, and consumed with self-pity. The heartbroken man is visited in jail by a vision of one whom he calls "Lady Philosophy," and she becomes his guide. Over the course of his book, Boethius learns that he had indeed suffered a great tragedy but that his greatest tragedy was not the loss of his reputation, wealth, or honor.

Boethius's guide leads him to see an even graver concern—one that it took this adversity to open his eyes to. Lady Philosophy shows him that his prosperity and his success, his victories and his gains, his personal glory and his public acclaim, had all led him to forget what is most important. Lady Philosophy leads Boethius to the realization that his "highest good" and "the hinge on which the greatest happiness turns"[3] is God. But the journey to this realization is a difficult one. We need God's help even to see God as our good. So Lady Philosophy sings a beautiful song asking for God's help—the God who brought forth the world out of his perfect love and in whose goodness all things have their good. She sings that the desire of every human being is to behold the majesty of God:

> To the blessed who alone behold
> it, you are the sole serene
> goal in which we may rest, satisfied and tranquil,
> and to see your face is our only
> hunger, our only thirst,
> for you are our beginning, our
> journey, and our end.[4]

Later, she sings, "How happy is mankind, if the love that orders the stars above rules, too, in your hearts."[5] Happiness is knowing and being known by the God of the universe.

This wise guide was not the first and neither will she be the last to sing this song. Many of our best artists, philosophers, and theologians throughout the centuries have defined happiness in this way. From Augustine to Aquinas, from John Calvin to Jonathan Edwards, from John Donne to John Owen, the definition of happiness is to know and delight in our Maker; it is to see God's face and so give him the glory he alone deserves (Isa. 42:8).

This is what we were made for, and this is precisely what we see throughout the Bible (Ps. 27:4; 105:4; 1 Cor. 13:12; 1 John 3:2). It is, in fact, the culmination toward which the whole biblical narrative builds. The book of Revelation ends with a picture of God dwelling with humanity. The end, quite literally, is communion with God (21:1–5). God's final intent is his original intent, and the unfolding story of the Bible describes the lengths to which God went in Christ to restore the communion that was lost in Eden.

If happiness is communion with God, no external event or circumstance can take this living hope away from us. That's what Boethius learned through what he suffered and lost. *Communion with God is humanity's highest privilege.* It is the great end to which all our teaching must point, to which creation and redemption are but the path.[6] "There is nothing on earth that I desire besides you. My flesh and my heart may fail, but God is the strength of my heart and my portion forever" (Ps. 73:25–26). But how can this song become our song?

Communion with God is happiness, Boethius learned. But how can we attain this communion? What words must we speak, what deeds must we perform, and what sacrifices must we make to reach this level of bliss? Some have thought that we can know God only by ascending to him through contemplation and purity or other efforts.[7] But God did not wait for us to become worthy and ascend to him. We cannot, for our sin separates us from him absolutely.

Instead, out of love God descended to become one of us.

THE STRANGE GLORY OF THE CROSS

Christians believe that Jesus reveals the character of God. John 1:18 says that Jesus has "made ... known" the God whom no one has seen or can see. The Greek word for "made known" is where we get our English word *exegete*, which means "to interpret" or "to explain." This is John's poetic way of saying that Jesus shows us God's character, and it is the ground of the distinctly Christian claim that "the glory of God" is revealed "in the face of Jesus Christ" (2 Cor. 4:6).

"It is a strange glory, the glory of this God," the German pastor-theologian Dietrich Bonhoeffer preached to a London audience in 1933.[8] God's divine glory did not appear in a way we would expect. Jesus entered the world not with the pomp and splendor of a ruling king but in humility, "taking the form of a servant" (Phil. 2:7), even washing feet (John 13:1–9). He practiced the way of faithful obedience all the way through suffering death, "even death on a cross" (Phil. 2:8), where he was finally given a crown and enthroned as a king with a sign over his head to prove it: "The King of the Jews" (John 19:19).

It's possible to read the gospel stories and conclude that Jesus' glory was in spite of the cross, that he endured the cross on his way to the *real* glory. But it would be more accurate, more biblical, to say that Jesus' glory was not in spite of the cross but through it. A strange glory indeed.[9] The cross was not *on the way to* glory but was integral to it, because the cross is where we see the fullest expression of God's self-giving love for us. God was most glorified when the Son of God was crucified (John 12:27–33).[10] This is a strange glory because it contradicts our expectations of what glory looks like and what God should be. As the apostle Paul observes in 1 Corinthians, the cross looks like foolishness to us. It offends our sensibilities. Yet this is exactly how God chose to reveal himself—not according to worldly wisdom but in the folly of the cross (1:18–21). Paul wrote these words to the church in Corinth, which was an ancient metropolis very much like Los Angeles, where we have written this book.

THE CORINTHIAN WAY

Corinth was a prosperous commercial crossroads, a port city located on a major east-west trade route. It had been sacked by Rome in 146 BC but refounded a hundred years later as a Roman colony. It was quickly repopulated with former slaves and freemen who saw in the new city new opportunities for social and economic advancement, opportunities not available in more settled cities like Rome. Hypersexualized and religiously pluralistic, it was home to dozens of temples, statues, and monuments, including a temple to Aphrodite, the goddess of love and beauty, on a high hill overlooking the city.

As a young city, Corinth was home to the upwardly mobile and those looking to make a fresh start. And because most of its citizens were not highborn, Corinth was very status conscious and status aware. People were obsessed with appearance, self-promotion and publicity, and given to boasting, which is why the word *boast* appears frequently in Paul's letters to that city.

Corinth was cosmopolitan, diverse in every way, materialistic, highly competitive, hungry for status, with an inflated emphasis on perception and recognition, resulting in widespread insecurity born of constant comparison. They even carved their names in the stones of the city in a desperate plea to be remembered.[11]

That was Corinth, but it sounds exactly like our city. The values of self-promotion and materialism and the practice of jockeying for power and popularity are deeply entrenched in the American way. It's all about what's bigger, newer, shinier.

THE WORD OF THE CROSS

To the community of Christ followers in that city, believers who had grown up swimming in Corinthian culture and values, Paul wrote the letter we call 1 Corinthians. A surface reading of the letter suggests the major issue confronting that church was disunity (1:10). But the deeper issue was that though they had heard the gospel of Jesus, their values and aspirations were still under the sway of their old Corinthian way. "Are you not being merely human?" Paul asks his readers (3:4). The saints in Corinth had more of Corinth in them than they had of Christ.

In effect, Paul is saying, "The gospel you have chosen to believe has not yet done its deep work. It has not captured your imaginations, the eyes of your hearts. You say you belong to Christ, but you are still living like Corinthians. You are still valuing what Corinthians value. You are still concerned about what Corinthians are concerned about. You are still measuring yourself against those old markers. You are still looking for status in all those old, merely human ways of success and power and wealth." Their real issue was continuing captivity to their culture's values, even within the church, and disunity was just the symptom.

We might wonder whether Paul was writing to ancient people or to us. Don't we still measure ourselves, compare ourselves, and seek status and recognition in all the old ways, as opposed to boasting only in the cross of Christ?

Yet the gospel, which Paul called "the word of the cross" (1:18), is actually promoting a whole new way of being—in Corinth or Los Angeles or wherever you live. Everything you once sought and valued must now be reinterpreted in light of the cross. That's what Paul was telling his status-seeking, competitive, anxious, and insecure readers. Christ's people are to model a new way of being human, where the old markers of success not only no longer count but also have been exposed as foolishness. So, what does the cross have to teach us about the art of living? For the apostle of the crucified Lord, the answer is *everything*.

We opened *The Cross Before Me* with Dr. Santos saying, "Our intuitions about what will make us happy ... are totally wrong."[12] But two thousand years before this professor spoke to her crowded lecture hall, the apostle Paul says virtually the same thing to a group of status-seeking Christians prone to boast in all the wrong things. Paul's point in 1 Corinthians is that the wisdom of God is to be found in the word of the cross.

God's way to the flourishing life, to the life that is truly life, is the cruciform way. We are prone to miss this, and we'd suggest that a Christian culture that prizes size, strength, and prosperity most often will miss it (and not just the obvious examples of prosperity preachers).[13]

Not only is the cross the instrument of human salvation; it is also the pattern for our lives here and now. The apostle Paul was saying in 1 Corinthians that the cross is more than a means of personal redemption—it shows us what it means to live a fully human life.

Where did Paul get such a counterintuitive idea? From the life and lips of his Master.

JESUS: TRUE GOD, TRUE HUMANITY

Jesus Christ, by his life, in his death, and through his resurrection, shows us what it means to live a fully human life. The Bible says that every human being is created in the image of God (Gen. 1:27). The Bible also says that Jesus is the perfect image of God (Col. 1:15). So when we wonder what it means to be created in the image of God, above all, Jesus shows us.[14]

Christians are familiar with the idea that Jesus shows us who God is. But seldom do we realize that Jesus also shows us what humanity was created to be.

Not only is Jesus fully God, but Jesus is also fully human. He is what the theologian Karl Barth once called "the real man."[15] Not only does Jesus show us what the proverbial real man looks like. He also shows us what Everyman, each man and each woman, was created by God to be. Jesus Christ defines the fully human life for everyone created in God's image—that is, for every human being.

"Not only do we know God by Jesus Christ alone, but we know ourselves only by Jesus Christ."[16]

If that weren't controversial enough, there's something even more challenging to our sensibilities. If Jesus shows us what humanity was created to be, then it's worth asking, *What character traits, ambitions, and values shaped Jesus' life? What does a fully human life look like?*

Jesus lived a life marked by humility. We don't typically associate humility with happiness or flourishing, yet Jesus tells us, "Learn from Me, for I am ... humble," and to this exhortation is attached a promise: "And you will find rest for your souls" (Matt. 11:29 NASB). Jesus could have selected any virtue for us to learn from him, for he possessed them all in perfect measure. But he singled out one above all. If we would find rest for our souls, then we must learn humility from him.

Jesus' life was marked by a compassion that placed the needs of others above self-concern. Compassion might sound okay, but if it means serving others in ways that inconvenience us, perhaps we would rather stay at home. Yet Jesus singled out compassionate service as the measure of a person's greatness. He told his self-seeking disciples that "whoever wishes to become great among you shall be your servant" (Mark 10:43 NASB).

Jesus deliberately eschewed fame and praise. We tend to be overly concerned with our reputations and care deeply what others think of us. Yet not only did Jesus ignore his reputation, but he "made himself of no reputation" (Phil. 2:7 KJV). It's not simply that he didn't seek the praise of others (John 5:44); he deliberately sought to make himself a person of no reputation. This is the very opposite of reputation building. It moves beyond self-forgetfulness to self-renunciation.

Above all, Jesus' life was marked by suffering, from start to finish. This is the most difficult pill for us to swallow, for who would consider suffering to be a defining feature of a good life? We actively avoid suffering. We prefer comfort. Yet Jesus was "a man of sorrows and acquainted with grief" (Isa. 53:3). He didn't deserve his suffering—it certainly wasn't a result of disobeying God. Instead, it was precisely his obedience to God that led him down a way of suffering, to "death on a cross" (Phil. 2:8). The Bible even calls Jesus' life of suffering "fitting" (Heb. 2:10), necessary for him to sympathize with us (4:14–15), and integral to his learning (5:8).

All these characteristics—his humility, compassion, service, renunciation of his will, and suffering—come together in the cross. Jesus' whole life was oriented toward a cross. He "set his face" toward it (Luke 9:51). "For this purpose I have come to this hour" (John 12:27). It wasn't just the culmination of his life; it was the *pattern* from start to finish. "His whole life was nothing else than a kind of perpetual cross."[17]

So if Jesus shows us life as God intended humans to live it, then we can see in Jesus' life that the way for a human life to flourish is the way of humility, compassion, service, and self-sacrifice. Happiness is found in the path of consciously making yourself of no reputation, even the path of pain and suffering. For Jesus this is the way to a fully human life: the way of the cross.

FINDING THE GOOD AND THE BEAUTIFUL IN THE CROSS

Ah, but does this sound like the good life to you? If we're honest, we would probably admit it sounds neither beautiful nor good. We might pay lip service and agree that the above virtues should be part of a good Christian life. But so few of us seem to believe that this path—what Thérèse of Lisieux once called the "little way"[18]—leads to the life we long for. If we did, our fears (what we are afraid of losing) and our ambitions (what we aspire to) would look very different.

We want to be careful to point out that this book is not a call to self-improvement. Jesus is not calling us to a new moral or religious program. He is calling us to himself. He has united us to himself if we belong to him. He is calling us to the fullest measure of life and happiness, of knowing and being known, of loving and being loved, of living in communion with him and his Father by his Spirit. This is the deepest fulfillment of our nature because this is what we were made for. Jesus blazed the trail, and his life shaped the path.

This book is also not about the imitation of Christ. Imitating Christ is impossible if our faith isn't grounded in our union with him. We press on into this new life from a position of confidence and security "in Christ," to use a frequent designation in the Bible of those who belong to Jesus. "Every spiritual blessing" is already ours if our lives are united to Christ (Eph. 1:3). We participate in Christ's life, death, and resurrection. If we are united to him, all that belongs to him now belongs to us. Imitation without participation is not life-giving. It's exhausting. It's just religious moralism.

This is a book about how we grow deeper and deeper experientially into the love of God. The way of the cross is not how we justify our lives before God. Jesus has already done that for us. This is a book about the way we move further up and further into this reality. It is not possible to make God love us more. But we can grow in our understanding of the love of God that's already ours.[19]

In terms of Boethius's story, didn't he already have the consolation of God's presence before he lost everything and entered that jail cell? Yes! But as Lady Philosophy pointed out, Boethius had forgotten who he was and what he was made for. It was only through his loss and deprivation, through his pain and humiliation, that he discovered what had been true from the beginning. It was when he saw God as the hinge of his happiness that he began to see clearly.

RIGHT-SIDE-UP THINKING

If we approach the way of Jesus as a moral, religious, or spiritual program to improve ourselves, we are bound to fail. It is a problem of motivation—that is, what moves the will. *Why* should we practice humility and service? Why be compassionate? Why be patient in suffering? Why pursue this cruciform life? If it's just a matter of following orders, this sounds like a pretty grim life indeed.

The best and truest reason for following the way of the cross is that it leads us to the deepest reality of things: Jesus and his kingdom. In being conformed to the cruciform life, we are being conformed to the very heart of God, a God of self-giving love. The entire world is a gift of that love. And the cross supremely reveals that love to us. The cross is the means by which "the love that orders the stars above," to quote Boethius, rules in our hearts.[20] This is the way—walk in it!

We can talk about the ways the cross turns our world upside down. It certainly does overturn our expectations. But in truth the cross actually turns the world right side up.

The cross shows us the rhythm of the way things were made to be. This is what C. S. Lewis in *The Lion, the Witch, and the Wardrobe* describes as "deeper magic from before the dawn of time."[21] The cross undoes the curse of sin and sets us free—free in relation to God, his world, other people, and ourselves.

As the cross invites us to reimagine the good life, it calls us to be displaced from the center of our own lives: the cross before *me*. And as we keep the cross before us, this vision renews our minds and transforms our wills until we see ourselves correctly. Humility, compassion, service, and self-sacrifice start to seem self-evident: *of course* this is what the good life looks like! And of course suffering is necessary to wean us from our self-reliance.[22] The cross tells the enduring true story of how new life comes. Only by losing our old way of life will we find new life.

By contrast, a life oriented around myself, with myself as my final goal, starts to show itself for what it really is: a distortion of the kind of life for which I was made. In this old way of thinking, *of course* the cross looks foolish to us. It looks foolish because *we* are foolish. Self-centered lives are sad and wasted lives. This offends us. It wounds our pride to hear that our very best, our greatest accomplishments, and our most sincere efforts often are moving us further away from a happiness we can rest in. This cruciform call offends us because, while we do want goodness and love, we want it on our terms.

Reflecting on why he believed in Jesus, the poet W. H. Auden writes, "I believe because He fulfills none of my dreams, because He is in every respect the opposite of what He would be if I could have made Him in my own image.… Why Jesus and not Socrates or Buddha or Confucius or Mahomet?… None of the others arouse *all* sides of my being to cry 'Crucify Him.'"[23]

The way of the cross is not the popular way. Thus, to write in praise of the cruciform life brings distinct risks. It can be easy to write about the cross in a way that is dour, grim, dark, pessimistic, life-denying. Perhaps that's why we often hear "Take up your cross" as a burden rather than an invitation. It can sound like a belittlement of life rather than its flourishing. This is why we need to begin with a clear sense of what the cruciform way is ultimately aiming at: flourishing—even joy!

Perhaps our reluctance is less because this way is asking too much of us and more because we expect too little of the new life God has for us. In his book *The Sickness unto Death*, Søren Kierkegaard writes, "There is so much talk about being offended by Christianity because it is so dark and gloomy, offended because it is so rigorous etc., but it would be best of all to explain for once that the real reason that men are offended by Christianity is that it is too high, because its goal is not man's goal, because it wants to make man into something so extraordinary that he cannot grasp the thought."[24]

The Christian story proposes something that is too high to believe. It's hard for us to believe that God could be so good that his glory and our joy could be intertwined, that, as the early Christian thinker Irenaeus puts it, "the glory of God is a human being fully alive."[25] Rather than tearing the human being down, the cross elevates the human being nearly beyond imagining.

A WISDOM CONTEST

We are not so different from the people in Corinth. We too are asking the way to the happiness we seek. We too are in a wisdom contest. We too are surrounded by competing stories of the good life and rival visions of happiness. All our public debates on hot-button issues are at their roots about how to flourish as human beings. And we are all participating in this contest through the choices we make and the values we prefer. This contest can be contentious, even overwhelming.

But this contest is perennial. Humans everywhere and at all times have looked for happiness. And throughout history we have sought it in familiar places: money, success, power, fame, health, beauty, and pleasure.[26] These can be good things in themselves, but they don't add up to happiness—not even when all achieved together (see Boethius). Our best wisdom teachers have long tried to tell us this, and scientists are now confirming empirically that our most common assumptions about what will make us happy are often entirely wrong.[27]

So what is the hinge on which all true happiness turns? Boethius discovered the song we need to hear again today: flourishing is found in God alone.

This book is about the distinctly Christian way to taste God's full and free life until we see his face. It is a strange glory, but it's the only way home.

THE SCANDAL
OF THE CROSS

Then and Now

*When the cross becomes a symbol of power or beauty, suppressing
the historical reminder of a particularly brutal instrument of
humiliation and death, then its own moral authority, under the
Christian rubric of "cross-bearing," is threatened.*

Philip Rieff, *The Triumph of the Therapeutic*

In 1983 the American novelist Walker Percy published a book
called *Lost in the Cosmos*. It bore the intriguing subtitle *The Last
Self-Help Book*. The self-help movement was in full swing, and
Percy found the phenomenon vexing enough to write the self-help
book to end all self-help books. He assembled a set of quizzes,

stories, and thought experiments—all standard content for a self-help book, but Percy used them for one specific purpose: to challenge the basic assumptions of self-help.

Percy showed that the self-help movement makes two flawed assumptions: we can really know ourselves, and we can truly help ourselves. Percy, a physician turned novelist and an adult convert to Roman Catholicism, was too astute to believe either. The self requires a cure more radical than any self-help book can provide.

We are especially susceptible to the promise of self-help—that a method, program, or technique will deliver reliable results on schedule. Modern science and technology have in many ways made us, in the words of René Descartes, "masters and possessors of nature."[1] More and more, we expect that this mastery should extend over our own nature.

At every turn, we find magazines, books, websites, and apps promising tips or techniques for improving our lives. We expect that the right method or life hack will allow us to master our careers, finances, health, bodies, relationships—in short, to master our*selves*. Whatever the problem, there's an app for that. We think, *The right combination of information and technology should allow me to fix whatever problem might arise.* And with technology advancing so quickly, our optimism seems warranted.

Yet amid the dizzying successes of our modern technological age, there is also a deep current of discontent. Technology, like any tool, can be a great blessing. But it can also make things too easy and convenient. Instant gratification has a way of devaluing our experience. Things don't seem to matter like they used to. So we find ourselves longing for things that have substance, that take time, that are more "authentic."

For some this means artisan breads and craft beers, wooden toys made by hand, vegetables grown in our own gardens. For others it means studying ancient wisdom for answers to modern problems and as a guide to happiness and the good life. Some are drawn to the wisdom traditions of the East: martial arts, yoga, Eastern philosophy, Sun Tzu's *The Art of War*. These seem fresh and real in comparison with Western ways of doing things. Others find the ancient Greeks and Romans to be a source of wisdom, whether in Spartan exercise regimens or attempts to live according to ancient philosophical schools, like the Epicureans and the Stoics.[2]

Today we may think of philosophy as an academic subject, but for the ancients philosophy was an art of living. As the French scholar Pierre Hadot put it, ancient philosophy was "a way of life."[3] We love that phrase, don't we? *A way of life.* Surfing is not just a sport; it's a way of life. Jazz is not just a style of music; it's a way of life. Fishing is not just a hobby; it's a way of life. The website for the Spartan obstacle-course races proclaims, "Spartan is more than a race; it's a way of life."[4]

The idea of a *way* suggests something that encompasses the full scope of how one lives. It is the self-conscious adoption of a particular manner of being. In Eastern philosophy and religion, the way, or Tao, connotes a kind of understanding that is not merely intellectual but must be lived. A way requires patient practice and submission to something deeper than the whims of the moment.

Yet at the same time, the idea of *a way* appeals to us because it suggests a project of self-creation, based on our personal choice regarding the shape of our lives. We love the modern ideals of self-creation, self-cultivation, and self-fashioning.[5]

There is a real tension between these two impulses: on the one hand, the impulse to follow a path that requires discipline and even submission to a standard deeper or higher than ourselves and, on the other hand, the impulse to decide freely what shape our lives will take.

What we want is a method of extracting the wisdom and principles from these ancient ways so they may be easily applied in consumer-friendly portions. We want the depth, meaning, and transformative power of these ancient ways, but we want to use them as tools to help us get what we want in life.

THE JESUS WAY

It may be easy to criticize some of these trends as fads, but we also need to take them seriously as symptoms of a deeper discontentment. They indicate a real need for meaning and depth. They indicate a genuine recognition of the superficiality of our modern culture of convenience and consumption. We are looking for a way.

It is significant that the earliest label for Christianity was *the Way*. Before Christians were called Christians, they were called followers of the Way (Acts 9:2). It is also significant that Jesus described himself as "the way" (John 14:6).

Yet many of us may not think of Christianity like this, as a way that encompasses our entire lives. If we do see Christianity as a way of life today, we often mean just whatever manner of living Christians share with those of similar social, cultural, and economic backgrounds. Our concept of human flourishing and the good life looks pretty much the same as that of our neighbors, except we go to church on Sunday and to heaven when we die. Otherwise, there is nothing distinctive about our way of life.[6]

If our lives don't look demonstrably different from those who don't claim to follow Christ, we have not really understood the Christian conception of flourishing. For Christianity is distinct in its idea that flourishing, happiness, and the good life can be found only by way of the cross.

THIS IS NOT A SELF-HELP BOOK

Percy's strategy in *Lost in the Cosmos* was brilliant: write a self-help book to critique the self-help movement. Someone ought to write something similar for the world of Christian publishing, where there is no shortage of books promising a method, technique, or pathway for reaching a spiritualized conception of success.

It is tempting for Christians to try to package the way of Jesus in a set of principles that will work for us. We find it in the preaching of the prosperity gospel, which promises us the good life—nay, our *best life*—now. We find it in books that suggest an ancient Hebrew prayer will help us break through to the blessed life. We find it in programs that show how to grow a thriving church.

This kind of gospel has been around in many forms for many years. Some are blatant, suggesting that God wants to bless us with riches and success. Other forms are more subtle, taking shape as the assumption that God exists primarily to give us what we want, to make sure we get the most out of our lives, relationships, and careers.[7]

In this regard, religious and spiritual books can lead us to the same predicament as self-help books. We want to tap into something that has meaning, depth, or spiritual significance. Yet we also want to make this spiritual source work *for us*, according to our notions of what makes for a good and successful life.

There is an endless supply of books that package the Christian story in this way. But this way is not the Christian story, because it leaves out something crucial: the cross. It is true that Jesus promised abundant life (John 10:10), but what does this abundant life look like? The Christian story suggests that this new life comes about only *through* the cross. We'd prefer a direct route or a shortcut to God's blessing, but the blessed life comes about only indirectly, via the death of the cross. This is the way of Jesus: "If anyone wishes to come after Me, he must deny himself, and take up his cross daily and follow Me. For whoever wishes to save his life will lose it, but whoever loses his life for My sake, he is the one who will save it" (Luke 9:23–24 NASB).

As we hope you've seen already, this is not another self-help book. Nor is it another book on Christian happiness. One of our claims in this book is that no book can give you a technique, system, method, or life hack to ensure you will flourish. There are no shortcuts: the cruciform life must be lived to be learned.

THE CROSS AS FLOURISHING?

Wait a minute. Jesus said that whoever loses his or her life for Jesus' sake will save it. Doesn't that mean he was promising that we will flourish, that we will be happy, so long as we first deny ourselves?

This might seem like a good deal, a sort of bargaining for God's blessing: I'll "give up" these things (wink, wink), and then God will give them back in greater proportion. But this idea of exchange assumes that we know what God's good blessings ought to be: health, an attractive spouse, financial security, comfort, career success, and more. These are not bad things. However, they are conspicuously absent from Jesus' description of blessedness.

In the Sermon on the Mount in Matthew 5, Jesus said the blessed ones are "the poor in spirit" (v. 3), "those who mourn" (v. 4), "the meek" (v. 5), "those who hunger and thirst for righteousness" (v. 6), "the merciful" (v. 7), "the pure in heart" (v. 8), "the peacemakers" (v. 9), "those who have been persecuted for righteousness' sake" (v. 10), and those who are reviled, are persecuted, and have evil spoken against them because of Jesus (v. 11).[8]

The Greek word for "blessed" here is *makarioi*. It can also be translated as *happy*, but that doesn't quite capture its significance. For the Greeks this word suggested the human being participating in the happiness of the gods.[9] Thus one recent translation renders it "blissful."[10] *Blissful* are those whose lives fit this description. Why? Because Jesus was describing the true heart of God—how God deals with the world and how his creatures ought to live in this world in light of God's coming kingdom.

Jesus was inviting his hearers into a new reality (more precisely, we could say Jesus was inviting us into reality—with which we have been living out of tune), one in which all things will be set right and God's creation and creatures will be renewed. This kingdom, the kingdom of God, is coming about not by way of power and might but through humility, weakness, and suffering love. Thus, the way into the reality of God's kingdom is by way of the cross.

This might seem like a bit of a stretch. For most of us this description of life doesn't sound much like flourishing. It sounds kind of miserable. It might even seem a bit dishonest, like a consolation for wimps and losers who can't get what they really want. Our world says that those who are strong, smart, or talented enough to get what they want must reach out and take it. How many times have you seen ads with a slogan or tagline that essentially says, "The meek shall not inherit the earth"?

What about those who are not winners? The world says, "Well, they can console themselves by rationalizing their failure: 'We aren't successful because we aren't that superficial. We don't care about money and success. We value higher things.'" To the winners it seems obvious this is just sour grapes.

To his credit, this is how Christianity appeared to Friedrich Nietzsche, one of the most psychologically perceptive thinkers of modern times. Nietzsche was raised a Christian but rejected Christianity, trying instead to reshape himself according to pre-Christian Greco-Roman sensibilities.

Nietzsche was a radical critic of Christianity, but Christians can learn much from his critique, which shows just how offensive the Christian message was to ancient ears (and should be to ours). This is true not only of the Christian picture of the blessed life but also of its relentless focus on the cross (1 Cor. 2:2). Worship a crucified God? Unthinkable. The cruciform life is the good life? Incomprehensible. Nietzsche writes, "Modern men, obtuse to all Christian nomenclature, no longer feel the gruesome superlative that struck a classical taste in the paradoxical formula 'god on the cross.' Never yet and nowhere has there been an equal boldness in inversion, anything as horrible, questioning, and questionable as this formula: it promised a revaluation of all the values of antiquity."[11]

Here Nietzsche, one of Christianity's most notorious critics, becomes one of our best teachers. He is correct that it is impossible for us today to appreciate how offensive the cross was to Jewish and Gentile hearers. We have become inured, such that the symbol of the cross retains little of that original offense. Crosses are everywhere—on churches, ambulances, and jewelry—to the point that the cross is in danger of falling into banality. If we are going to understand the radical cure, the truly good news, of the Christian way, then we need to reckon with why the cross was such a scandal in the ancient world.

Our interest is not, however, merely historical. We need to recover that sense of scandal so we can better understand why the cross should strike us as offensive today. The cruciform life may be counterintuitive, but in this chapter we want to go beyond the merely counterintuitive to recover a genuine sense of *scandal*, because it is only when we grasp the offense of the cross that we are really able to understand what it means and why its conception of human flourishing is such good news.

THE SCANDAL OF THE CROSS IN THE ANCIENT WORLD

The cross was a stumbling block to the people in the ancient world. In 1 Corinthians 1:22–25, the apostle Paul writes, "Indeed Jews ask for signs and Greeks search for wisdom; but we preach Christ crucified, to Jews a stumbling block [*skandalon*] and to Gentiles foolishness, but to those who are the called, both Jews and Greeks, Christ the power of God and the wisdom of God. Because the foolishness of God is wiser than men, and the weakness of God is stronger than men" (NASB).

The cross was an offense to Jewish believers expecting a triumphant messiah. The notion of a crucified messiah was incomprehensible to them. It seemed a contradiction in terms, like an aged newborn or a cowardly hero. The idea of an executed messiah was contrary to all of Israel's hope for a coming king who would liberate them from their oppressors and restore Israel to its proper place.

We see this throughout the gospels. Jesus' disciples had no category for understanding his claims that he would be crucified and resurrected. Thus, when it happened, the cross appeared to spell the end of any hopes the disciples had that this man could be the messiah. In their eyes the cross was a decisive defeat. As proof, despite the fact that Jesus had told them "plainly" that he must suffer and then would rise again (Mark 8:32), no one was camped out at the tomb, waiting for Jesus to come back to life.

The idea that the Christ, the anointed one, would achieve his victory through a gruesome death was inconceivable. For Jesus' Jewish contemporaries, his crucifixion would have been the surest confirmation that God was not with him. According to Deuteronomy 21:23, God's curse is on anyone who is hanged on a tree (see Gal. 3:13).

The cross was just as offensive to Greek and Roman sensibilities. "Greeks search for wisdom," Paul reminds us (1 Cor. 1:22 NASB), and their conception of wisdom was not shaped like a cross. For the philosophers, wisdom meant knowing the nature of things: the cosmos, the gods, the principles of nature, and the place of human beings in this order. Wisdom consisted in contemplating this order. For the Greeks, contemplation was the highest human activity—the activity that brings us closest to the divine.

The basic assumption was that human beings need to *ascend* if they are to come close to the divine. The Greeks and Romans assumed that if there were going to be any meeting of gods and mortals, it must take place with the lower rising to the level of the higher. This assumption matched the social hierarchy of antiquity: those of higher status did not descend to meet those below.

The cross shows us a God who upset humanity's ideas and highest ideals about the natural hierarchy.[12] Christianity introduced a startling new idea of God into the ancient world. Here was a God who became human. Unprecedented. Sure, there were plenty of pagan myths about gods masquerading as humans, but those ruses were all selfishly motivated, with the gods pretending to be human in order to carry out whatever agenda they might have at the moment. The Christians told a story in which God became human out of love for human beings, to save them. This kind of downward mobility was unimaginable to the ancients.[13]

For Plato and his students, God is the good—perfect, unchanging, eternal. It was inconceivable that the eternal would or could come into time, the immaterial into the material. As Plato put it in *The Republic*, "Does anyone, either god or human being, willingly make himself worse in any way at all?" For Plato, to be a god is to be "as fair and as good as possible," so it's simply "impossible ... for a god to want to alter himself," but instead he would remain "forever simply in his own shape."[14] For Platonists, the incarnation—the Word made flesh and dwelling among us (John 1:14)—was beyond offensive. It was inconceivable. Yet Christianity proclaimed a God who took on flesh, not as a mere mask, pretending to be human, but by becoming fully human. He was born of a woman and made himself of no reputation (Phil. 2:7), living the life of a servant in the backcountry of the Roman Empire, via Nazareth (John 1:46).

For the Greeks and Romans, wisdom was also knowing how to live—that is, how to pursue the good life, to live well and be happy. One of the main priorities of ancient Greek and Roman civilization was the pursuit of the good life. The goal of Greek and Roman politics was to create a state in which the good life would be possible. This meant providing a setting of political stability, material prosperity, and leisure in which citizens could pursue happiness.[15] Those who threatened the stability of the state were the ones executed by crucifixion.[16]

In short, just as the Jewish observer would have seen the cross as a sign of God's curse, for the Gentile observer, crucifixion was no less definitive as a negative judgment on one's life and actions.

For everyone in the ancient world, the cross was a very public display, a demonstration of Rome's power and judgment: *this* is what happens to the enemies of Rome.

The cross was the most notorious means of public execution. Some have suggested that the ancients wearing a cross as jewelry would be like us wearing a tiny electric chair. Bad taste, to say the least. But this analogy doesn't quite get it right.

As Fleming Rutledge points out, the electric chair is typically a fairly private affair, and it is meant to be over as quickly as possible. The opposite was true of the cross. It was a very public affair, meant to put the enemies of Rome on display as an example. It was also meant not to be over quickly but to drag on for an excruciating length of time.[17]

In addition to inflicting pain, it was meant as a mark of public shame. No one would want to be associated with a crucified criminal. Russell Moore remarks that the shame of crucifixion was something like the shame we associate with being on the sex-offenders list.[18] No one would want to have anything to do with you. As Rutledge observes, the goal of crucifixion was nothing short of the complete annihilation of the person. The cross was about reducing a person to nothingness, to a nonentity.[19]

In summary, the cross was inappropriate to mention in polite company. It's not surprising, then, that the cross did not appear in Christian art for the first few centuries of the church. The scandal and horror of crucifixion were too fresh and familiar to be a subject of artistic depiction. It is all the more surprising then that the apostle Paul appealed to the cross as the focal point of his theology. In his first letter to the Corinthians, he wrote of his determination "to know nothing among [them] except Jesus Christ and him crucified" (2:2). This is Paul's theology of the cross.

THE THEOLOGY OF THE CROSS

As we have seen, in the ancient world the cross was nobody's idea of the pathway to flourishing and the good life. The cross perennially upsets our ideas of how to pursue happiness. Jesus ascribed bliss to those who are not typically praiseworthy: the meek and the merciful, the persecuted and the poor in spirit. The Beatitudes (Matt. 5:3–11) are not just clever turns of phrase meant to challenge our thinking. They are little sticks of dynamite to blow up our conception of what makes for a blessed or blissful or happy life.

The Greeks and Romans would have had a difficult time understanding the vision of the good life that Jesus and Paul laid out. The philosopher Alasdair MacIntyre observes, "Aristotle would certainly not have admired Jesus Christ and he would have been horrified by St. Paul."[20]

The apostle Paul made the cross the center of his theology, showing how the cross of Christ requires a total reconfiguration of the way we think about what it means to be human and what it means to live well, to do good, and to know God. The cross requires what the biblical scholar Richard Hays memorably calls "the conversion of the imagination."[21] Instead of showing himself in glory and power, God revealed himself in humility and weakness. This is the theology of the cross.

Historically the phrase *theology of the cross* was made famous by Martin Luther in his *Heidelberg Disputation*. Luther made a key distinction between two basic ways of doing theology: what he called the "theology of glory" and the "theology of the cross." These are rival ways of thinking about God, two models for talking about who God is and how we come to know him.

Luther did not, however, invent the theology of the cross. He derived the idea from the apostle Paul. Instead of trying to make the message of the cross attractive with a veneer of power and wisdom, Paul emphasizes its weakness and folly. The cross shows us a God who was not content to sit in eternal bliss, indifferent to the condition of humanity, like the gods of the Greeks and Romans. The cross shows a God who became human, who lived a life of humility and service, and who chose to suffer and die. How else could this message be heard by ancient people but as lunacy? "The word of the cross is foolishness to those who are perishing, but to us who are being saved it is the power of God. For it is written, 'I will destroy the wisdom of the wise, and the cleverness of the clever I will set aside.' Where is the wise man? Where is the scribe? Where is the debater of this age? Has not God made foolish the wisdom of the world?" (1 Cor. 1:18–20 NASB).[22]

The word of the cross is a direct challenge to the theology of glory, which appeals to the wisdom of the wise and the strength of the strong. The theology of glory prefers good works to suffering, strength to weakness, wisdom to folly, and, in short, glory to the cross. The error is subtle because it uses religious language. It speaks of God and the things of God. It is a theology.

The theology of glory appeals to our sensibilities. And it says true things: that God cares about what is good and beautiful, that God wants us to be strong and wise. But these are most dangerous half-truths because they leave out the most crucial aspect of reality: that God cares about the good, the beautiful, the strong, and the wise according to his own terms. The glory and greatness God cares about are on God's terms, the God who revealed himself in Christ and the cross.

Today the theology of glory takes many forms. These forms are so familiar to us and so highly valued by our culture that we may not recognize them as theologies of glory. But they need to be exposed in order for us to recapture our sense of the scandal of the cross.

THE THEOLOGY OF GLORY TODAY: REASON

Reason is a good gift and is to be used wisely. But like all our natural gifts, it is meant to serve God. It turns bad when it tries to become self-sufficient. The fool is "wise in his own eyes" (Prov. 26:12). When human reason takes itself for its own standard in deciding who God is or ought to be and how one comes to know God, it is foolish.

The theology of glory takes reason to be a ladder that ascends into heaven, a tower of Babel by which humans try to reach God on their own, seeking "to force an entry into heaven."[23] Reason wants to determine what God's attributes are: infinite, immortal, eternal, unchanging, all-knowing, all-powerful, perfectly good. And there is some basis for this in Romans 1, where Paul writes, "His invisible attributes, namely, his eternal power and divine nature, have been clearly perceived, ever since the creation of the world, in the things that have been made. So they are without excuse" (v. 20). This is why Greek philosophers were able to reason out some things about God that agree with Scripture.[24]

The danger is to assume that reason is sufficient to give us the whole story about God. Our reason, our rational perception of things, is prone to mislead us, insofar as it is unwilling to accept who God has chosen to be for us in Jesus, the crucified carpenter from Nazareth.

Human reason *can* get some things about God right. But Romans 1 shows how our reasoning about God can stray into idolatry: "Even though they knew God, they did not honor Him as God or give thanks, but they became futile in their speculations, and their foolish heart was darkened. Professing to be wise, they became fools, and exchanged the glory of the incorruptible God for an image in the form of corruptible man and of birds and four-footed animals and crawling creatures" (vv. 21–23 NASB).

Instead of worshipping the living God, the peoples of the world turned to idols. The inner logic of idolatry is that it aims to make God visible, controllable, and thus available to our own agendas so we can bend reality to our wills. Idolatry occurs when we want to make God our instrument, the means by which we can achieve our own ends. The theology of glory doesn't renounce God. It wants to *use* God to give us that which we think we really need to be happy, significant, and secure.[25]

THE THEOLOGY OF GLORY TODAY: PROSPERITY

The theology of glory is an idolatrous theology. It can take the form of idolatrous reason, but it also takes other forms. One of the more conspicuous is the prosperity gospel.

It can be overt: God wants you to be rich! A recent poll of Protestant Christians who attend church at least once a month found that 69 percent agreed with the statement "God wants me to prosper financially."[26] But more often the prosperity gospel takes subtler forms—not so egregious as claiming God wants us to be healthy and wealthy per se, but that what God wants lines up pretty well with what we want, and what we want lines up pretty well with our culture's idea of success. Or the idea that if we're prospering professionally or materially, then God must be blessing us.

Christianity Today editor Mark Galli observes how common it is among evangelicals to support this by appealing to subjective experience with phrases like "I have a peace about this ...," "God showed me …," or "I felt the Spirit's leading …" Galli writes, "I've lost count of the number of stories I've heard about God 'opening doors' or giving one 'peace' about buying a larger home or uprooting our families to take a better-paying job." Galli says that in all his years he has "almost never heard an evangelical Christian say" that God told him or her, "Sell your possessions and give to the poor," despite the fact that Jesus says that very thing in Luke 12:33.[27]

Financial prosperity and career success are not intrinsically bad things. Like any other created thing, they are gifts of God to be received with gratitude. But like the rest of creation, they can become idols when we seek in them our happiness, security, or sense of worth and meaning.

They also become idols when we take these visible things as a measure of God's favor. So many Christians think that if they are successful, then God is pleased with them. If they fail or suffer in some way, then the implication is that God is displeased with them.[28]

That is the theology of glory, and it is everywhere in the American church.

A theologian of the cross, on the other hand, sees suffering as a sign that God is healing our distorted vision, our mistaken views of who he is and how he works. *How could this be God?* we wonder. This view of suffering requires a revolution in our way of knowing.[29] In Moses' great sermon in Deuteronomy 8, he said that material prosperity without humility is fatal, often requiring painful discipline as a sign of God's fatherly care for our souls (vv. 2–5;

see Heb. 12:5–6). Prosperity is its own trial and has been the ruin of many lives.

THE THEOLOGY OF GLORY TODAY: SELF-IMPROVING AND SELF-MAKING

The theology of glory assumes that the pathway to God is one of making ourselves better, whether through the moral law, ethical formation, or spiritual practices. This is another manifestation of the theology of glory: self-making.

How do we justify our existence? What bestows meaning and worth on our lives? How do we gain recognition before others— whether God or other people? The theology of glory holds that we justify our existence by what we do. "Be somebody!" "Do something with your life!" We have different ideas of what it means to be somebody or do something significant. It might be career success. It might be moral righteousness or ethical virtue. It might be having the right positions on the right issues. It might be fame or honor. It might be performance or publications. It might be health, beauty, or fitness. It can look like the desire to make an impact and leave a legacy, even for Christ.

Advertising, of course, makes millions by heightening our anxieties about these things. A few years ago the sportswear company Nike (aptly named after the Greek goddess of victory) ran a campaign with a striking slogan: "Make Yourself." The slogan had several extensions: "I'm making myself strong," "I'm making myself shine," and "I'm making myself proud." Their social media campaign spelled out this vision in more detail: "You are entirely up to you. It's your body. Your life. And you're in charge. You're working hard to Make Yourself unbeatable. Unstoppable. The best. But sometimes your best only gets you so far. Click 'Like' above to go beyond your best. To inspire and be inspired. To declare how you're Making Yourself to women everywhere. Click 'Like' to become a Nike Woman."[30]

If you aren't inclined to create yourself in the image of the Nike woman, there are plenty of other options. A rugged frontiersman, for instance. Budweiser recently had a billboard in honor of such individuals: "For those who write their own stories ..." (this Bud's for you).

The logic here is that you are what you make of yourself. You justify your own existence by what you do. You make yourself right by doing righteous actions, as you define what is righteous. So be a good person, as you define good. Stand up for good causes. Make good decisions. This logic is entirely conditional: my meaning and worth depend on how well I do.

But the word of the cross introduces a radically different logic that says we are incapable of justifying our existence. We are made right by an unconditional gift of God. Prior to anything we did, God chose us and adopted us as his own. Instead of requiring that we make something of ourselves, *God makes something of us.*

We see this in Paul's letter to the Corinthians. Instead of flattering his hearers, citing their distinguished backgrounds and accomplishments, Paul does the opposite: "For consider your calling, brothers: not many of you were wise according to worldly standards, not many were powerful, not many were of noble birth. But God chose what is foolish in the world to shame the wise; God chose what is weak in the world to shame the strong; God chose what is low and despised in the world, even things that are not, to bring to nothing things that are, so that no human being might boast in the presence of God" (1 Cor. 1:26–29).

God makes something of us through his free gift of Christ's work on the cross. In the cross and resurrection, Jesus defeated sin, death, and the Devil in order to reconcile us to God. God does everything. It is all of grace, but this gospel of grace offends our self-justifying hearts, because we're hell-bent on trying to prove ourselves—or to at least contribute something. Anytime we want to add anything to the gospel (which is almost all the time), we are exposing ourselves as theologians of glory, still inclined to boast in something besides the cross alone (Gal. 6:14).

THE THEOLOGY OF GLORY TODAY: SPIRITUALITY

One other prominent version of the theology of glory is what is nowadays often called "spirituality." This is a vague term that often encompasses many good things, like spiritual disciplines and spiritual formation. We will have more to say about this in chapter 9.

But the term *spirituality* also encompasses many dangerous things, particularly when it indicates more of an exploration of the self than a genuine encounter with God. In this sense of the term, spirituality is not so much about devotion to a reality that transcends us and asks something of us but is instead about deepening our experience, awareness, and self-actualization, often through meditation.[31]

It may seem fresh, but this is a long-standing idea in American religious life, from New England transcendentalists to academic gnostics to an army of self-help gurus and secular life coaches. The common theme is that God is found not in the empty formalities of traditional institutional religion but in our most intimate experience of ourselves. God is not outside, beyond, or other than us; the true God is found within, in our own spiritual awareness.[32] The fundamental principle of this theology of glory is that God is ultimately identical with our deepest selves.

Like the idolatry of other theologies of glory, this kind of spirituality tends to instrumentalize God. Our relation to God becomes a means to our own self-actualization or happiness. This is part of a broader cultural shift toward thinking in therapeutic categories. Our culture's highest ideal is self-realization, not self-*denial* in service of a higher commitment. The goal of life, culture says, is simply to get the most out of life.[33]

What is lost in this shift is the meaning of ideas like sin, judgment, and the cross. Why did Jesus have to die? It's not clear what the cross has to do with the drama of *my* life. The old religious vocabulary of sin has been replaced by a psychological vocabulary. We may acknowledge that we are broken, but we hesitate to say that this is because *we* have broken the moral or divine law.

Yes, we are broken. But we are broken not only because of some tragic flaw in our constitution. We are broken because we are in revolt against God. We need healing, but we also need to recognize that each of us is, in the words of John Henry Newman, "a rebel [who] must lay down his arms."[34]

This is an uncomfortable truth that the cross confronts and exposes. Our condition in sin is far worse than we realize. The condition of the world in revolt against God is far worse than we realize. But God's love is also greater than we realize. God was willing to go to the cross to reconcile the world to himself (Rom. 8:32). The cross reveals God's love for humanity. *And* it reveals humanity's hatred of God. The cross is God's judgment of a world in revolt against its creator. But instead of punishing the guilty, Christ bore our sin.

These concepts of sin, divine judgment, and the cross offend our therapeutic sensibilities. But this offense, this scandal, is necessary, not simply to tear down the therapeutic self-help complex. Too often the resistance against the therapeutic turn in Christianity is to deny it outright with sayings like "God is not interested in your happiness, only your holiness." But this kind of talk is just the other side of a false dilemma.

The cross is, in fact, divine *therapeia*, the cure for our disordered souls and the source of genuine human flourishing. We become our true selves *through* the cross. The problem with the therapeutic turn in Christian preaching and teaching is that it makes God nothing more than the means to our flourishing. God is not the means. God is the end. He is not merely the way to happiness. God *is* our happiness. Seek God, not happiness! Our flourishing lies in God. The cross is the way to this end.

THE WAY OF THE CROSS: COMMUNION AND HUMAN FLOURISHING

There is much to critique, lament, and ultimately reject in these theologies of glory. They encourage a kind of narcissism or vanity that makes the self and our projects the center of reality. This is the sense in which theologians like Augustine and Luther described sin as "incurvature" (the self curved in on itself). This is the self that must die (Mark 8:34) and that we should hate (John 12:25), the self that seeks its glory through its own reason or its own doing, which Paul calls the "old self" (Eph. 4:22). This self must be crucified.

But we do need to appreciate the way this incurvature and these projects of glory are distortions of a fundamental human need. All human beings need to be recognized. We need to be seen, known, and loved. Repeatedly in Genesis 1, God created and saw that it was good (vv. 4, 10, 12, 18, 21, 25, 31). We are creatures who need to hear, from God and from significant others, "It is good that you *are*." That is what we hear in the cross. No matter how deep our sin or how severe our revolt against our creator, God is *for* us, and he showed us this on the cross. This is how far God was willing to go to reconcile us to himself.

The problem with these theologies of glory is not that they are too glorious. Ironically, they are not glorious enough. They do not

THE CROSS BEFORE ME

see the true and beautiful surpassing glory of who God actually is. Nor do they grasp the true glory of who human beings are created to be. We seek our own glory through our projects, trying to be or make ourselves into something that is meaningful and worthwhile. But these projects pale in comparison with what God is actually doing and what we were actually made for. We want to be the heroes of our own stories, but our stories are paltry in comparison with the story God is telling.

At the cross, God is inviting us into his bigger story. It is the story of the creation of the cosmos. It is a grand epic of revolt and redemption and reconciliation. Not by might or power but by self-giving love—a God who became human and died on a cross to redeem us. It is a story of new creation brought about by resurrection from the dead, and this story tells of a promised fulfillment in "a new heaven and a new earth" (Rev. 21:1–5). This vision is unspeakably glorious.

And you, dear reader, were made to be in this story. In Christ your destiny is to participate in this story, to know and be known by your creator. This is the communion for which you were made. This is the home for which you're longing. The only way into this story, however, is by way of the cross. That's not the fine print of the contract—that's the way to the life of glory because that's the heart of the God of glory.

The cruciform life means giving up our self-salvation projects. It means letting go of our stories as we have always understood them. It means giving up our old sense of who we are and what we thought our lives were about.

Dying to yourself is a painful thing. Taking up our crosses offends our natural sensibilities. Of course it does!

This is the heart of the cruciform life. Real flourishing comes only through the cross. This means dying to the illusion that we are the center of our lives. We do not find ultimate meaning in ourselves. But in giving up these false ideas of ourselves, we don't become less ourselves. We become *more* ourselves. We are set free from ourselves to become our true selves by becoming part of the grand story of God and the world.

CRUCIFORM WORK

The Crucifixion of Personal Ambition

Ingmar Bergman is considered one of the greatest film directors to have ever lived. He grew up as the son of a Lutheran minister in Sweden, and though he abandoned the faith of his childhood, the films he made were profound explorations of the big questions of existence: love, death, and God. Bergman once wrote an essay about his creative process and what he was aiming for with his films:

> People ask what are my intentions with my films—my aims. It is a difficult and dangerous question, and I usually give an evasive answer: I try to tell the truth about the human condition, the truth as I see it. This answer seems to satisfy

everyone, but it is not quite correct. I prefer to describe what I would like my aim to be. There is an old story of how the cathedral of Chartres was struck by lightning and burned to the ground. Then thousands of people came from all points of the compass, like a giant procession of ants, and together they began to rebuild the cathedral on its old site. They worked until the building was completed—master builders, artists, labourers, clowns, noblemen, priests, burghers. But they all remained anonymous, and no one knows to this day who built the cathedral of Chartres.

Regardless of my own beliefs and my own doubts, which are unimportant in this connection, it is my opinion that art lost its basic creative drive the moment it was separated from worship. It severed an umbilical cord and now lives its own sterile life, generating and degenerating itself. In former days the artist remained unknown and his work was to the glory of God. He lived and died without being more or less important than other artisans; "eternal values," "immortality" and "masterpiece" were terms not applicable in his case. The ability to create was a gift. In such a world flourished invulnerable assurance and natural humility....

Thus if I am asked what I would like the general purpose of my films to be, I would reply that I want to be one of the artists in the cathedral on the great plain. I want to make a dragon's head, an angel, a devil—or perhaps a saint—out of stone. It does not matter which; it is the sense of satisfaction that counts. Regardless of whether I believe or not, whether I am a Christian or not, I would play my part in the collective building of the cathedral.[1]

What might work done for the glory of God look like today? Bergman is writing about his own creative process but his parable could be applied to any of our vocations. Our work should not be about distinguishing ourselves in our fields or being remembered for our craft. Think of all those unnamed artisans of varying skill—master builders and clowns—laboring away for months on end in some obscure corner of that old cathedral, some crevice high up and hidden to the human eye, some niche no one else would ever see, much less praise. Yet the work was done with meticulous precision, not for personal recognition but in complete anonymity, for the satisfaction of a job well done and for the eyes of one.

So we too, in whatever work we set our hands to do, are artisans of differing gifts and varying skills called to work in different corners, some obscure and some not, contributing our craft in the collective building of some grand cathedral. It's not about being recognized. It's the satisfaction that comes from playing our small part, without comparison, as our Master assigns to each one of us. We must learn to say in our work, "Master, I'm here to do your bidding. Every talent I've been given is from you and for your glory. So I surrender the results of my best efforts to your wise providence."

Chapters 1 and 2 established that God's wisdom for human flourishing is paradoxical. Brené Brown comments that the etymology of the word *paradox* is instructive. *Paradox* is the joining of a Greek prefix and verb, *para* ("contrary to") and *dokein* ("to appear or to think"). The Latin *paradoxum* means "seemingly absurd but actually true."[2] It seems not only counterintuitive but also absurd to claim that the way up is down, that difficulty can be the way to peace, that the abundant life comes about by the broken way. Carl Jung puts it, "Where you stumble and fall, there you find pure gold."[3]

But it's not enough to notice paradoxes. Wisdom requires that we learn to live by them.

This can seem especially difficult in a city like Los Angeles. How does the cruciform life appeal to a crowd bent on working hard and doing things excellently? For those striving to distinguish themselves in their respective fields, the notion of the cruciform life gets an almost immediate reaction: "Are you saying we should stop striving or trying to do our best? Are you implying we should be content with mediocrity?"

If we want to think about the cruciform life as God's wisdom for human flourishing, one of our first questions is, *What, then, about my work?* After all, that's where we spend many of our waking hours.

More specifically, we might also ask, *What about ambition?* Is there a place for ambition in the life of self-denial to which Christ calls us? If so, what might ambition shaped by the cross look like? If everything, including our work, must now be reinterpreted in light of the cross, what might the crucifixion of our career aspirations look like? How is this life-giving, because it doesn't sound life-giving, does it?

AMBITION RECONSIDERED

If you're the driven sort—a self-motivated, type A, naturally competitive person—you may have thought about this question before. The artist Salvador Dalí said, "At seven I wanted to be Napoleon. And my ambition has been growing steadily ever since."[4]

Or perhaps you do not think this theme applies to you. Perhaps you don't consider yourself to be the ambitious sort and you're suspicious of those who appear to be. But it's not just the obviously achievement-oriented among us who must come to terms with ambition.

"Ambition," John Stott writes, "concerns our goals in life and our incentives for pursuing them. A person's ambition is what makes him 'tick'; it uncovers the mainspring of his actions, his secret inner motivation."[5] By Stott's definition, ambition is not a contemptible thing; it's a human thing. It's part of our being creatures who desire. Ambition is inevitable because motives are unavoidable. In fact, we are all ambitious, each one in his or her own way. We can't help it, nor should we be ashamed of it.

Moneyball by Michael Lewis is the story of how Billy Beane, a small-market general manager for the Oakland Athletics, changed the way major-league baseball is played and how players are valued. Before Beane, professional baseball teams looked at a lot of stats to determine a player's value: batting average, home runs hit, slugging percentage. Beane's breakthrough was that only one number really mattered: wins. And how do you win? You score more runs than your opponent. And how do you score runs? You get on base. What baseball statisticians call "on-base percentage" is the key.

Moneyball is a story we love—a pioneer who is willing to look foolish for a time but who perseveres and changes the system by his courage to question the status quo. In the climactic scene of the book's film adaptation, Beane, played by Brad Pitt, is talking to the owner of the Boston Red Sox, and the owner tells him, "This is threatening not just a way of doing business, but in their minds it's threatening the game. But really what it's threatening is their livelihood. It's threatening their jobs. It's threatening the way that they do things."[6]

If you became a Christian or began to take your faith seriously as an adult, this sense of threatening how you've always done things may feel familiar. Alongside a wonderful sense of a new discovery, there is also a feeling that can only be described as disorienting, even traumatic. You discover that what Billy Beane did for baseball, Jesus has done for your life. He threatens your whole (old) way of life and calls into question how you've always done things. Jesus turns your motivational structure upside down by calling into question why you're doing what you do. And the overturning of your motivational structure is disorienting, to say the least.

When I (Rankin) became a Christian, I was in my early twenties. One question that plagued me was, "What am I supposed to do now with all this drive? Isn't ambition about seeking glory for oneself?"

In his gospel John artfully conveys that each one of us is ambitious. Seven times in chapter 12 John mentions "glory."[7] Everyone in the scene is, in one way or another, pursuing glory, even Jesus. The key line is verse 43, where John does something unusual for the biblical writers: he pulls back the veil on the characters' innermost motives. John reveals that some of the authorities believed in Jesus but, fearing how their public profession of faith would affect their status and reputation, had decided to keep their faith a private matter. John lays their hidden motives bare: "They loved the glory that comes from man more than the glory that comes from God."

That verse is as profound a diagnosis of human motivation as any in the Bible. Another translation reads, "For they loved the praise of men more than the praise of God" (KJV). That's the bottom-line question of human motivation: Whose glory are you seeking? Whose praise? Because—make no mistake—we are living for glory; we can't help it. But whose glory?

Ambition—we could no sooner be rid of it than be rid of ourselves. The question is not, "Are you ambitious?" The question is, "What does your life show that you are ambitious for?"

AMBITION CORRUPTED

The most often forgotten of the seven deadly sins is *acedia*, which is often translated "sloth." But in its ancient context, *acedia* didn't mean "laziness." It conveyed a condition of listlessness, a spiritual torpor, a lack of concern with one's spiritual condition, a lack of hungering after God. For the ancients this lack of spiritual drive was deadly. This spiritual drive is good and necessary to living in God's way.

The serpent in the garden of Eden, before the fall of Adam and Eve in Paradise, played upon the noble and natural dignity of human aspiration: "Ye shall be as gods" (Gen. 3:5 KJV). This shows that ambition was a part of our original created nature in Eden. To aspire to what is good and glorious is part and parcel of what it means to be a human fully alive.

Yet our ambition has been corrupted. What is corrupted ambition? In one of his essays, C. S. Lewis captures the distinction with characteristic clarity:

> Ambition!… It isn't wrong for an actor to want to act his part as well as it can possibly be acted, but the wish to have his name in bigger type than the other actors is a bad one.…
>
> What we call "ambition" usually means the wish to be more conspicuous or more successful than someone else. It is this competitive element in it that is bad. It is perfectly reasonable to want to dance well or to look nice. But when the

dominant wish is to dance better or look nicer
than the others—when you begin to feel that if
the others danced as well as you or looked as nice
as you, that would take all the fun out of it—then
you are going wrong.[8]

Paul puts it this way: "Do nothing out of selfish ambition"
(Phil. 2:3 NIV). His statement is as challenging as it is blunt, since
most *everything* we do is fueled by this desire to promote ourselves,
often vis-à-vis others. When ambition becomes tied to comparison, Lewis says, our ambition becomes corrupted.

In the spring of 1814, Timothy Dwight, the president of Yale
College, gave a baccalaureate address to Yale's graduating class. But
this was not your typical dare-to-take-the-road-less-traveled com-
mencement speech. Dwight's address was entitled "On the Love of
Distinction."[9] He began by acknowledging that distinction has an
appeal for all. Who doesn't wish to stand out in the eyes of others?
Yet he warned the graduates, "Selfishness is in its nature little and
base. But no passion, and no pursuits, are more absolutely selfish
than the love of distinction…. How terrible must be the account,
given of life, spent only in labouring to acquire distinction….
Among all the passions, which mislead, endanger, and harass, the
mind, none is more hostile to its peace, none more blind, none
more delirious, than the love of distinction."[10]

These days nothing seems more common or less terrible than
the appeal to stand out and be recognized. *Be yourself and publicize
it!* Yet this love of distinction, this selfish ambition, is not God's

wisdom, wisdom from above. It is wisdom from below marked by "envy and selfish ambition," which the Bible calls not only "unspiritual" but also "demonic" (James 3:14–16 NIV). Whoa!

If we try to carve out our own significance, "Look at me!" it's bound not only to exhaust us but also disintegrate and dehumanize us, as it has done from the beginning. We become less than who we were made to be when we try to make ourselves great.

But you can see the tension: we are irrepressibly ambitious, yet our ambitions are unfailingly distorted.

Can our ambition be healed? Yes. But for our ambition to be healed, it must sooner or later, gradually and almost always painfully, be crucified. This is how we will be set free from the corruption of our ambition: by the crucifixion of our ambition.

AMBITION CRUCIFIED

This crucifixion usually happens in the place where our ambition is most clearly revealed—our work, our calling, how we spend our time and passion. Whether you're a stay-at-home parent, teacher, coach, writer, doctor, or real-estate broker, the crucifixion of your ambition happens through the crucifixion of your calling.

For example, Rankin is a pastor. The healing of his ambition will come through the crucifixion of his ministry. That's the title of a book by Andrew Purves: *The Crucifixion of Ministry*. The subtitle catches the idea: *Surrendering Our Ambitions to the Service of Christ*. Purves says this surrender comes by way of the difficult, slow-dawning awareness that you must be displaced, painfully displaced, from the center of your own ministry to the point where you realize "It's not my ministry."[11] My life calling belongs to Jesus. It's Jesus' ministry.

One might think this challenge applies more to pastoral ministry than to business or finance, but Rankin was a corporate banker before he became a pastor. It's hard to pursue the crucifixion of your ambition in any environment that encourages and rewards precisely the opposite. No matter your career, you must be displaced from the center. Otherwise you'll never be able to loosen your grip. Our desire for distinction, to justify our lives by the work of our own hands, is too strong.

Purves says that this displacement means the death of "*my* ministry," and he likens this process to a crucifixion.[12] He was writing as a seminary professor, but a Christian CEO of a tech firm could just as credibly write a memoir with the same subtitle: surrendering your ambitions to the service of Christ. Somewhere along the way, you stop climbing the ladder you were on and begin climbing another mountain.[13]

Crucifixion is a hard word. But it's good news for your working life because, as it was for Jesus, it remains the path to a new life, to a freedom and joy that no accomplishment, no gain in your work could ever give you. Contentment will never come by way of achievement—that's the illusion that has to die.

Crucifixion is an apt metaphor, because in the ancient world crucifixions were not only devastatingly painful but also slow and public! That was part of the torture—you didn't die quickly, and you couldn't control the timing. It was humiliating because everyone could see what was happening to you. You were stripped.

Exposed. You were even denied the dignity of a quick execution. People who were crucified died of asphyxiation when they were finally so weary, so sapped of strength, that they could no longer even lift their chests to draw another breath.

Painful. Slow. Humiliating. No control. Surrender.

No matter our calling, we must be displaced from the center. And Purves adds the warning that the more talented and gifted we are and the more competent we imagine ourselves to be, the more painful will be our crucifixion.[14]

Finding your identity in Christ means learning to look outside yourself to Jesus to tell you who you are. No longer is your identity what you do or how others see you, but it becomes what Jesus has done for you and how he sees you.

It's one thing to agree theoretically and abstractly: my life is not about me. It's another for this truth to take root in the soil of your heart so you can withstand storms at work and push beyond the thorns of worry that seek to choke out the new life (Mark 4:7, 18–19). Like all biblical knowledge, this knowing has to be lived to be learned. But when we finally glimpse that our worth is in Christ, not in our work, we no longer have to worry about being remembered for what we've done or how others view us.

It's glorious that one thief asked Jesus, "Remember me when you come into your kingdom" (Luke 23:42). This is a prayer for all who can admit that we too have stolen glory from God. But it is even more glorious that long after everyone who knew you is gone, long after no one is left who has heard your name, long after the stars on the Hollywood Walk of Fame have crumbled into dust and the mountains have tumbled into the sea, there will be one who promised never to forget your name: "Can a woman forget her nursing child, that she should have no compassion on the son of her womb? Even these may forget, yet I will not forget you" (Isa. 49:15).

It's easy to imagine that we can grasp this benefit without actually having to go through this crucifixion. Or it's natural to hope that the crucifixion of our ambition can be over quickly. Yet as we've said, one of the most difficult parts of crucifixion is that we are not in control of the timing! But while we wait for God to do his deep work, there are some ways for us to consider whether our ambition is in the process of being healed.

THREE TESTS OF AMBITION

The first test of ambition: *Are you content in your work?* Contentment is the best gauge of whether your ambition is selfish or crucified. When your plans or your dreams have not panned out or when life, particularly in the area of your greatest gifting and passion, has not turned out the way you expected, how is your contentment? This is a test, a crucible.

There is such a thing as a holy discontentment. This is when you look out on the world and see that things are not as God would have them. You feel compassion or even a kind of righteous indignation rising up in you, causing you to fight for justice, bring deliverance to the captive, and yearn for wrong to be made right.

But more often than not, our discontentment signals that there was more to our ambitions than noble aspirations. When things were going our way, it was easy to tell others, even ourselves, "This is not about me. It's for God." But our real motives get exposed when our hopes are dashed or our plans get frustrated.

If your work really is for the glory of God, you can do your best and trust the results to God. When personal ambition is being healed, you are learning to be content in plenty and in want (Phil. 4:11–12) because you have surrendered the results to God's good and wise providence. The pain you feel at releasing the results in the face of disappointment is the pain from the crucifixion of your selfish ambition. "Blessed is the man whom you discipline, O LORD ... to give him rest from days of trouble" (Ps. 94:12–13).

Second test: *How do you face failure or being seen by others as weak and ineffective?* In *The Way of the Dragon or the Way of the Lamb*, the authors argue that leaders in the evangelical church may preach a message of relying on Christ alone but more often than not our ministry and methods suggest we are relying on our own gifts and measuring success by counting and comparing.[15] While being interviewed for that book on Jesus' path of power, J. I. Packer says, "In the Christian life and in ministry, weakness is the way. The way of weakness ... has two aspects. One is that the watching world sees you as weak in the sense of being limited and inadequate. The second aspect is that you yourself are very conscious of being limited and inadequate."[16]

Packer doesn't pretend that weakness is simply a posture assumed for ministry effectiveness. No, you will feel weak, he says, and others will see you as limited and inadequate. A sign of your ambition being healed is that you no longer fear experiencing this feeling or having that reputation. You press into it. You boast in your weakness (2 Cor. 11:30), as opposed to feeling as if weakness is something to hide or a problem to overcome or as if being seen as inadequate is a narrative that you need to refute.

We hope this is a consolation if you are feeling that you are a failure in your work or that you have been overlooked or have not lived up to your own expectations. Thank God that he crucifies our reliance on what we can do so that we too can sing, "The LORD is my strength and my song, and he has become my salvation" (Ex. 15:2). It's so painful, but as there was for Jesus, there is for us a new life waiting on the other side of this crucifixion of our reputations.

Third test: *Do you celebrate the accomplishments and successes of your peers, especially those in your field?* Lewis says this is where our ambition goes awry—not the desire to dance well, but the desire to dance better or to be seen as better. Do you feel that the success of another somehow diminishes you? When your ambition is being healed, you no longer envy or resent others who are better than you at what you do best. You compare yourself only to increase your appreciation and respect for them. You can be second and be satisfied. Like Bergman's workers on the cathedral, you can even be unseen and be satisfied, because no matter what the organizational chart says, you know whom you are working for.

The movie *The Natural*, based on the novel by Bernard Malamud, is the story of a baseball prodigy named Roy Hobbs (played by Robert Redford). Hobbs is a great player, but just as it seems he's destined for fame, his dream is snuffed out by a vindictive young woman named Harriet Bird (played by Barbara Hershey).

Early in the film she asks him why he plays baseball. He says he wants to be so good that "when I walk down the street, people will look at me and say, 'There goes Roy Hobbs … the best there ever was.'" Harriet asks, "Is that all?" But Hobbs doesn't understand her question.

A day later, just before his major-league tryout with the Chicago Cubs, Harriet calls Hobbs to her hotel room and shoots him with a silver bullet. Sixteen years pass, and Hobbs finds his way back into baseball and eventually reunites with his childhood sweetheart, Iris (played by Glenn Close).[17]

Though film buffs and sports fans remember the film for its iconic closing scene of Hobbs hitting a dramatic home run to win the pennant, the best line from *The Natural* may be what Iris tells Hobbs (in Malamud's novel): "We have two lives, Roy, the life we learn with and the life we live after that. Suffering is what brings us toward happiness."[18] Roy Hobbs's career was crucified. His ambition was cut short, but it brought him happiness on the far side of "Is that all?"

EXCELLENT WORK

Roy Hobbs wanted to be "the best there ever was." Yet it was only by losing this dream that he found his happiness. Is the lesson that we shouldn't try to be the best? Where does this leave the drive for excellence? Should we just settle for mediocrity and not try too hard? What does this look like *concretely*?

It is worth noting the ways we use the word *best* in everyday language. Roy's desire to be "the best there ever was" is a desire to be recognized as better than everyone else. His motive is to achieve not excellence per se but only in rivalry with others. This is different from the desire to be your best or to do the best job you possibly can—to do or make good things because they are *good*.

The drive to do excellent work is a manifestation of our role as God's image bearers in the world. Humans are what J. R. R. Tolkien calls "sub-creators,"[19] and there is a sense in which it is appropriate that, like our Maker, we recognize the merits of work well done and judge it good.[20]

The pride, however, of "*I* did that!" is not appropriate. We are not God creating things *ex nihilo*—out of nothing. We are using abilities God has given us and materials God has provided. "What do you have that you did not receive?" (1 Cor. 4:7). When we see our gifts in this light, we can recognize what is good in our work and have gratitude to have participated in making something. We can rejoice in excellent work—without seeing it as a means of glorifying the self—because it glorifies God to make things that are good and beautiful.

We opened this chapter with Bergman's story about anonymous craftsmen laboring on a cathedral they would never see completed in their lifetimes. Their work was not about being recognized or remembered. The work itself became an act of worship—doing the very best work possible in order to glorify God.

Is it possible to look at our work and say, "It is good," without being arrogant? Yes. True humility is the ability to delight in our gifts without attaching our egos to our work. C. S. Lewis makes this point in *The Screwtape Letters*, writing that God wants a person to be able to "design the best cathedral in the world, and know it to be the best, and rejoice in the fact, without being any more (or less) or otherwise glad at having done it than he would be if it had been done by another."[21] This is the posture of cruciform work: not to make things so our names will be remembered but to create beautiful things because beautiful things are good and because they reflect the glory of God.[22]

We will return to this theme of humility in the next chapter. For now there is another very practical question to address. We've given some tests of ambition, and we've seen that ambition to do good is not a bad thing, but how can our ambition be healed so it can be rightly ordered as God intends?

THREE PATHS TO OUR AMBITION HEALED

In the gospel of John, Jesus says, "How can you believe, when you receive glory from one another and do not seek the glory that comes from the only God?" (5:44). How can you believe the gospel—the good news that God's approval alone matters and his approval can never be earned by our works but is always a gift of grace received by faith—when we are still seeking the approval of others and trying to earn it by the work of our hands?

As we say throughout this book, the way to healing is the way of the cross. The way to have your ambition healed is to crucify it. There are three roads to our ambition being healed.

The first road is the way of failure, even humiliation. In a little essay entitled "The Uses of Humiliation," François Fénelon writes,

> What a mercy humiliation is to a soul that receives it with steadfast faith! There are a thousand blessings in it for ourselves and for others, for our Lord bestows His grace upon the humble....
>
> Our faults, even those that are the most difficult to bear, will all be of service to us if we make use of them for our humiliation without relaxing our efforts to correct them. It does no good to be discouraged. That is only the result of a disappointed and despairing self-love. The true method of profiting from the humiliation of our faults is to see them in all their deformity without losing our hope in God and without having any confidence in ourselves....
>
> We must hope for nothing from self, but wait for everything from God. Convicted of our helplessness, we have no confidence in ourselves, and yet we have unbounded confidence in God....
>
> Those who are truly humble will be surprised to hear any kind of praise given them. They are calm and peaceful ... merciful and

> compassionate … quiet, cheerful … incapable of
> strife. They always take the lowest place, rejoice
> when they are despised, and consider everyone
> better than themselves. They are lenient to the
> faults of others in view of their own. They are
> very far from preferring themselves before any-
> one. We may in this way judge our progress in
> humility by the delight we have in humiliations
> and contempt.[23]

Failure and humiliation are shortcuts to healed ambition. You've probably heard someone say, "I wouldn't wish what I've gone through on anyone, but I wouldn't trade what God has taught me for anything."

A second route to crucified (and thereby healed) ambition is daily death, the most common and most accessible path. We'll develop this more fully later in the book, but here's a preview. You may have heard the saying "Eternal vigilance is the price of freedom." It's another one of those paradoxes—the way to be free in your work is to be eternally vigilant against that which corrupts your ambition. Every time envy rears its head and says, "What about me?" and every time the ego tries to exalt itself and says, "Look at me!"—this is an invitation to put your self-centeredness to death.

A third path to the crucifixion of ambition we could call the way of Ecclesiastes. You get everything you ever wanted, and you discover it isn't enough. You climb one mountain only to discover there's nothing at the top—or at least not what you were expecting. That doesn't eradicate your ambition but does redirect it to another mountain, what Malamud calls "the life we live after,"[24] or what David Brooks calls "the second mountain."[25]

A FINAL PORTRAIT OF CRUCIFIED AMBITION

Patient zero of ambition healed is the apostle Paul. By all accounts, before he became a disciple of Christ, Paul was a most ambitious man and wildly successful. He gives his résumé in his letter to the Philippians (3:4–6). He came from the right kind of family, went to the best school, had a great job, and had a sterling character and reputation among his peers. But something happens to Paul, something traumatic. He encounters the real Jesus on the road to Damascus (Acts 9:1–20).

What happens next is almost always overlooked, but after that encounter with Jesus, Paul spends fourteen years we're not even sure where (Arabia?), doing we're not sure what. But perhaps he was trying to answer questions like "What now? What will this mean?"

Take comfort in those fourteen years. While Paul's salvation encounter on the Damascus Road was instantaneous, his understanding of what it would mean for his life and calling took many years to coalesce. It took years for Paul to say, "I have learned to be content" (Phil. 4:11 NASB). And this was the apostle Paul! But if his ambition could be healed, so can ours.

He says about his ambitions, his accomplishments, "I counted [them] as loss for the sake of Christ" (3:7). It's fascinating that Paul renounces not his failures but his successes. He counts his former wins as losses. His badges of distinction, his trophies, the very things he had been pursuing, were keeping him from recognizing what he truly needed. "I count everything as loss because of the surpassing worth of knowing Christ Jesus my Lord" (v. 8). Knowing Christ is superior to every other ambition he had ever had.

Paul learns that loving the glory that comes from God means loving above all the one in whom that glory is found (2 Cor. 4:4). In speaking of his ensuing death on the cross, Jesus says, "Now my soul is troubled, and what shall I say? 'Father, save me from this hour'? No, it was for this very reason I came" (John 12:27 NIV).

And then listen to the next line: "Father, glorify your name" (v. 28 NIV). Jesus' primary ambition is to bring glory to the name of God. Then a voice thunders from heaven, "I have glorified it, and will glorify it again" (v. 28 NIV). And how would God glorify his name again? Jesus says, "'And I, when I am lifted up from the earth, will draw all people to myself.' He said this to show by what kind of death he was going to die" (vv. 32–33).

We are accustomed to speaking of Christ's death as his humiliation and of the cross as the necessary prelude to glory, as in the saying "No crown before the cross." But John's gospel makes clear that Christ's glory came not on the far side of the cross but on it, not in spite of the cross but through it. This is the great paradox of glory in the gospel of John: the cross *is* the glory of God. The most detestable, gruesome act—nailing a man to a stake of wood—is the way this promise to Moses was finally fulfilled: "I will make all my goodness pass before you" (Ex. 33:19).

Jesus' life shows us why the way of the cross is still the way to live for the glory that comes from God. When we grasp how good our God is and that he died for the very ones who would steal his glory, we can't help but love the glory that comes from God more than the glory that comes from people.

This is how Paul could redirect all the ambition that used to oppose the gospel and come to say, "I make it my ambition to preach the gospel, [but] not where Christ has already been named" (Rom. 15:20).

Knowing Christ doesn't lead to mediocrity. It doesn't quench our ambition; it purifies it.

John Stott puts it, "Ambitions for God … if they are to be worthy, can never be modest. There is something inherently inappropriate about cherishing small ambitions for God. How can we ever be content that he should acquire just a little more honour in the world? No. We long to see him crowned with glory and honor and accorded his true place, which is the supreme place."[26]

You don't need to leave your job for your ambition to be healed. Healed ambition means no longer being undone by criticism, no longer being frightened to fail or to look weak or incompetent. You handle success lightly. You might even count it as a loss. Above all, today and again tomorrow you surrender your ambitions to God's good providence and rest in the gospel. You go to work tomorrow, working *from* approval not *for* approval. That's crucified ambition.

HUMILITY AS THE HEART OF THE CRUCIFORM LIFE

The first product of self-knowledge is humility.

Flannery O'Connor, "The Fiction Writer and His Country"

Lord Jim, a novel by Joseph Conrad, is the story of a young British seaman named Jim, who becomes first mate on a ship full of pilgrims heading to Mecca for the hajj. In the middle of one night, disaster strikes their ship at sea. The hull is ruptured, causing the vessel to take on water. It begins to sink slowly while all the passengers remain asleep.

Jim pauses at this crucial moment and decides not to stir the whole ship awake. Knowing there are not enough lifeboats to save all the passengers, the captain and crew decide to save themselves and steal away in the night. Jim goes with them, leaving the pilgrims to their watery grave.

The next evening, Jim and the crew are rescued, and they fabricate a story about their escape, only to discover that their abandoned ship and its passengers have also been rescued. The captain and crew evade the court of inquiry, leaving Jim to face the charges alone.

He's devastated by his cowardice and overwhelmed with shame. Before this, Jim considered himself to be daring, brave, and idealistic, thoughtful of others. He was first mate on a boat full of pilgrims, an admirable young man! But this moment of testing revealed his true character to himself and the world. He's devastated by this new self-knowledge.

Conrad's novel is a classic story because it conveys a perennial theme: the story of someone trying to come to terms with what he's done and can never undo. Jim has discovered something about himself that he doesn't like and perhaps the worst horror is the realization that it was true about him even before this pivotal moment. It took a crisis to reveal what was really inside his heart.

Conrad's narrator says of Jim, "It is my belief no man ever understands quite his own artful dodges to escape from the grim shadow of self-knowledge."[1] But it's not just Jim. We all work very hard to hide the truth about ourselves from ourselves and from others. Humility, it has been said, is reality. It's coming to see ourselves as we truly are before God, and this revelation is always wounding. We stand exposed before the world, as Jim did, and we wonder how we will ever get over the grim self-knowledge Conrad describes.

Jim was humbled, and being humbled is painful. But as Julian of Norwich puts it, "First there is the fall, and then we recover from the fall. Both are the mercy of God."[2] This introduction to ourselves is God's mercy. At first and for longer than you can stand it, being humbled doesn't feel like kindness. It feels like death. But just as the way of the cross was the doorway to a new life for Jesus, so it is for us. And the way of the cross is always the way of humility.

Jesus reveals to us that humility is the heart of the cruciform life.

A thousand years ago, Bernard of Clairvaux wrote a treatise, *On the Steps of Humility and Pride*, in which he comments, "Christ had all the virtues. But although he had them all, he especially commended one of them to us in himself (Rm 5:8), that of humility, when he said, 'Learn of me, for I am meek and lowly of heart' (Mt 11:29)."[3] He could have chosen any virtue, for he possessed them all in perfect measure, but Jesus singled out humility as the primary one we are to learn from him.

Jesus gave us an example of humility by kneeling before his disciples and washing their feet. Yet humility wasn't just something Jesus modeled (John 13:14–15). Humility is how God appeared to us in Jesus—humility is who Jesus is. "He humbled himself" (Phil. 2:8). To become like him, therefore, is to learn to walk in his path. In calling us to humility, Jesus calls us to himself.

Humility might not seem the most attractive virtue. We might want to be courageous, wise, and just ... but *humble*? We need to reimagine humility so we can get a glimpse of how beautiful and desirable it really is.

IN PRAISE OF HUMILITY?

Humility is a difficult idea to define. Maybe the best way to start is by noting how striking it is that Bernard would write a book in praise of humility. In the ancient world almost nobody valued humility. Humility was not only not valued, it was actually spoken against.

Greco-Roman society was a shame-and-honor culture, where nothing mattered more than your family's honor and your own status and reputation. For example, Aristotle describes the best sort of man not as one who is humble but as one who exhibits *megalopsychia*: literally, "greatness of soul." The great-souled man is noble, not small-minded. He concerns himself with great things. He is worthy of these great things, and he knows it.

This is not vanity, which is a person thinking he or she is greater than he or she really is. No, for Aristotle this is true self-knowledge: the great-souled man knows himself to be worthy of great things. The great man knows his own greatness, and he acts accordingly. He enjoys honor from those who are fit to honor him, but he despises honor from those beneath him. He does good things for others— not so much for their sake but because this is the sort of thing that a great man does. It is a way to display his true superiority.[4]

In the ancient world greatness of soul was the crown of the virtues. It allowed one's excellence to shine. Therefore, prizing humility would have been inconceivable. But something happened to change that. Something happened to make humility not only beautiful but also essential to the good and beautiful life.

God became a human being.

Unlike the Greek and Roman myths, this was not a god temporarily masquerading as a human. Jesus was fully God and became fully human. The eternal entered time; the infinite entered the finite. "Though [Jesus] was in the form of God, [he] did not count equality with God a thing to be grasped, but emptied himself, by taking the form of a servant, being born in the likeness of men. And being found in human form, he humbled himself by becoming obedient to the point of death, even death on a cross" (Phil. 2:6–8).

Because of Jesus, humility became central to the Christian vision of the good life. Who could have claim to *megalopsychia* more than Jesus? He's the creator of the universe, aware of his own greatness, worthy of great honor. Yet Jesus humbled himself to display his greatness and glory.

For the first time in human thought, the way of excellence was depicted as a path that led downward. This would have scandalized Aristotle and the classical great-souled man. And this scandal continues to offend our modern sensibilities. Yet Jesus says there is one thing above all that he wants his followers to learn from him: humility (Matt. 11:29).

To the point that four centuries later Augustine wrote that there are three things essential to grasping the truth about God, "The first part is humility; the second, humility; the third, humility."[5] Fourteen centuries after that, Andrew Murray wrote, "Humility … is … the first duty and the highest virtue of man. It is the root of every virtue."[6]

If we want to live life according to God's wisdom, a fully human life, then we must follow Jesus on the path of downward mobility, even—especially—in an upwardly mobile world that prizes self-esteem and promotes self-expression and self-aggrandizement. To praise humility is still to swim against the current—a current that runs not only outside us but also inside us.

Humility is a fight. And if you want it, you have to come to see it as the fight of your life.

HUMILITY: A DEFINITION

So what is humility? At its heart, humility is a form of self-knowledge. The German philosopher Dietrich von Hildebrand defines it as "the habit of living in the truth."[7] Humility is a recognition of the way things really are. It is a recognition of the truth about ourselves in relation to God, creation, and other people.

What, then, is this truth about ourselves? It's a staple of the Christian tradition that knowledge of God and knowledge of ourselves are intertwined. We can't know who we are without knowing God, and we can't know God without knowing something about who we are. In that sense, humility simply means knowing our place before God. That's Bernard of Clairvaux's definition: "Humility is the virtue by which a man recognizes his own unworthiness because he really knows himself."[8]

Talk of unworthiness is out of vogue today, seen as old-fashioned and possibly even dangerous in the face of soaring rates of depression. What's replaced it in the last century is C. S. Lewis's oft-quoted idea of humility as self-forgetfulness: not thinking less of ourselves but thinking of ourselves less. "If you meet a really humble man ... he will not be thinking about humility: he will not be thinking about himself at all."[9] It's interesting that Bernard, writing eight hundred years before Lewis, agrees that self-forgetfulness is the epitome of humility. But he goes on to remark that this level of humility is altogether so rare and so difficult to achieve that we should begin with a more accessible rung on the ladder of humility: a sense of our own unworthiness.[10]

If we start by denying ourselves, we may end with forgetting ourselves, but the way to get there is by way of a realistic self-assessment. "Humility," one writer says, "does not consist in criticizing yourself, wearing ragged clothes, or walking around submissively wherever you go. Humility consists in a realistic opinion of yourself, namely that you are an unworthy person."[11]

Humility is making a bit of a comeback today. It is even touted as an essential ingredient of great CEOs.[12] But most often it's defined in such a way as to take out any hint of lowering oneself. This might explain why humility's cousin, vulnerability, gets the most press today. Vulnerability is a wonderfully important part of humility. But true humility goes beyond vulnerability to reckon with truthful self-knowledge.

Pride is untruth. Falsehood. It is important to acknowledge this because otherwise it can be easy to suppose that humility and pride aren't really that big of a deal. We have begun to think that they're comparable to having good or bad manners: you should be humble because it's bad form to be overly pleased with yourself. Nobody likes a braggart. But pride is not a surface-level issue. It goes to the heart of our entire existential orientation. It concerns the very essence of who we are, and often the surest sign of pride is the belief that we aren't proud. "If anyone would like to acquire humility, I can, I think, tell him the first step. The first step is to realise that one is proud. And a biggish step, too. At least, nothing whatever can be done before it. If you think you are not conceited, it means you are very conceited indeed."[13]

The struggle against our pride is worth fighting because our pride will blind and bind and destroy us. The author Beth Moore writes that pride aims to cheat us of all that is good and beautiful in life:

> My name is Pride. I am a cheater.
>
> I cheat you of your God-given destiny ... because you demand your own way.
>
> I cheat you of contentment ... because you "deserve better than this."
>
> I cheat you of knowledge ... because you already know it all.
>
> I cheat you of healing ... because you're too full of me to forgive.
>
> I cheat you of holiness ... because you refuse to admit when you're wrong.

I cheat you of vision ... because you'd rather look in the mirror than out a window.

I cheat you of genuine friendship ... because nobody's going to know the real you.

I cheat you of love ... because real romance demands sacrifice.

I cheat you of greatness in heaven ... because you refuse to wash another's feet on earth.

I cheat you of God's glory ... because I convince you to seek your own.

My name is Pride. I am a cheater.

You like me because you think I'm always looking out for you. Untrue.

I'm looking to make a fool of you.

God has so much for you, I admit, but don't worry ...

If you stick with me
You'll never know.[14]

Pride postures itself as seeking the good of the self, but it actually leads to bondage and destruction. Humility, however, opens us to all the good things that are closed to us by our pride. Pride is falsehood; humility is truth, and the truth will set us free. This is why humility is central to the way of the cross and central to the good life. We won't seek humility, much less prize it, until we grasp that Jesus' humility is not life-denying but life-giving.

As Rankin's wife said to him once, after he voiced another grievance about his circumstances, "There are not too many problems you face that a little humility won't solve."

Once you believe the cross really is God's way to the good and beautiful life, then instead of fearing what humbles you, you can remind yourself, "Anything that humbles me is good for me." Not good as in eating your broccoli, but good as in *Thank you, God, for revealing my faults and weaknesses, for allowing me to face setbacks and disappointments. Thank you for anything that humbles me, anything that moves me closer to the freedom and truth of seeing who I really am and who you really are. Anything that humbles me is good for me, because it leads me toward joy in you, not away from joy.*

Humility does not diminish life; it leads us to it. When Jesus says, "I am the way, and the truth, and the life" (John 14:6), he is saying that the way to life is his way, the way of the truth of humility. That's the life on the far side of Conrad's grim self-knowledge. Humility gives our souls the rest that our achievements never could. As Jesus promises, "You will find rest for your souls" (Matt. 11:29).

SEVEN TRUTHS ABOUT HUMILITY

In what follows we lay out seven vital truths about humility before God. Each is followed by a brief exercise, a way to practice what Jeremy Taylor calls "the grace of humility."[15] Humility is a gift from God, but we can increase it by practicing it.

1. Humility is a grateful recognition that we are finite creatures.

When we are young and life is going well and we are at the peak of our abilities, it is easy to feel that we are invincible. We forget that we did not bring ourselves into existence and that we cannot preserve our own existence. At every moment, we are upheld by God. We are entirely dependent. We are nothing in ourselves.

But because of God's creative love, we are something: creatures. And as creatures there is nothing we have that we have not received (1 Cor. 4:7). *Humus*, the Latin root of *humility*, means "earth."[16] Our bodies come from the dust of the earth, and for a span of time between two dates on a tombstone, we borrow this dust. The breath in our lungs was breathed into us by God.

Our entire being is a gift. Humility is rooted in gratitude for this gift.[17]

> *Exercise:* Meditate on 1 Corinthians 4:7: "What do you have that you did not receive?" Consider all that you have received, give thanks to God for these gifts, and ask God how you can serve others with them. Then consider the gifts God has given others. Make a habit of thanking God for them. Thank God for upholding your existence even now, for your very breath.

2. *Humility comes from recognizing our fallenness.*

Humility is the sober recognition not only that we are finite, frail creatures but also that we are fallen. When we feel as if we are doing all right at behaving ourselves and staying out of trouble, it is easy to suppose that most of us are basically good and decent folk. We might even fancy ourselves to have the potential for heroic deeds under the right circumstances. And some of us might.

But we would also do well to remember Conrad's *Lord Jim*, who collided with the ugly truth that we also have the potential for great cowardice, even evil.

Many of us will never face such a dramatic moment of personal reckoning, but for those who do, it is a devastating experience. Consider Peter, who "broke down and wept" (Mark 14:72). We want to be proud of ourselves and have no regrets. We prefer to assure ourselves that in similar circumstances we would have acted more heroically than Jim did.

But ask yourself, *Have I really loved God with all my heart, soul, and strength? Have I really loved my neighbor as myself?*

Kathleen Norris observes that some hymnals have changed the lyrics to "Amazing Grace" to say that grace is amazing because it saved not "a wretch like me" but "someone like me." The word *wretch* has fallen into disfavor since it sounds too harsh. Wretch? Maybe some people are wretches but surely not *me?* To which

Norris replies, "It seems to me that if you can't ever admit to being a wretch, you haven't been paying attention."[18]

What is the point of dwelling on our wretchedness? It is essential to truly knowing ourselves, and for that reason it is essential to true humility. In our therapeutic age, it's this sense of unworthiness when face-to-face with God that we need to recover. Don't we find this at the cross? As Bonhoeffer puts it, "The cross is God's truth about us, and ... when we know the cross we are no longer afraid of the truth."[19]

At the cross we find the truth about who we are before God. In ourselves we are wretched and dead in our sin and in revolt against God. But in Christ we are forgiven and reconciled to God. Humility is rooted in knowing both our worth and our unworthiness.[20]

The cross shows us both.

> *Exercise:* Confess your sins. Name them. Acknowledge them to God, but also make a habit of confessing to others. While private confession is good, confessing to a friend or confessor helps reveal sin for what it is. It is humbling to say out loud or write down what we have done or left undone. Find a mature, trustworthy friend so you can confess to each other on a regular basis and receive assurance of forgiveness in Christ.

3. Humility is rooted in confidence.

Sometimes humility gets confused with a lack of confidence. This is a distortion because what is most often underneath our lack of confidence, sometimes expressed as self-pity and self-contempt, is not true humility but wounded pride, a wounded self-love. We thought we were better than this? That's pride. Thomas Merton has a wonderful phrase for this self-loathing that is full of self-pity. He calls it the "humility of hell."[21]

The cross shows us our true worth. The cross declares our fixed value in the eyes of God. Jesus died for sinners such as you and me. True humility is not the absence of confidence—it's grounded *in* our confidence. Humility is not timidity. It is trust and confidence in who we are in Christ: beloved and worthy, gifted and talented.

One of the most genuine tests of humility is your ability to name and delight in your particular gifts and how you respond when you are praised (Prov. 27:21). To delight in our gifts without resting on them or using them to prop ourselves up—this is the confidence of true humility. All human beings possess an undying need to be known, to be seen and recognized, for others to see us and say, "It is good that you *are*." In short, we want to be loved, even praised and esteemed.

Pride distorts this desire, making us desperate to be seen and affirmed. Pride seeks this esteem both from itself and from the world. As a result, pride is fragile and makes us fragile creatures. Humility, by contrast, has no urgent need for recognition from the world, because you know you are seen, known, and loved by God.

You do not have to do anything to secure or justify your existence. In Christ, you are loved and forgiven unconditionally by God prior to anything you do. In Christ, God justifies your existence, and he will establish you.

> *Exercise:* Preach the gospel to yourself daily. Remind yourself of this truth: I am in Christ, and Christ is in me. That is the base from which I live and act. I am already loved. My existence is already justified before I do anything.

4. Humility is moved by love.

How can we tell the difference between the false humility of wounded pride and the true humility of trust in Christ? True humility is moved by love. It loves and moves toward others because it knows it is loved by God. This is why Paul's letter to the Philippians appeals to Christ's example when it exhorts us to "do nothing from selfish ambition or conceit, but in humility count others more significant than yourselves. Let each of you look not only to his own interests, but also to the interests of others" (Phil. 2:3–4).

When we do this, we are following the example of Jesus, who—because of his love for human beings—took the form of a servant (vv. 5–7). His downward path was a descent of love. Therefore, when we are moved by his love, we are willing to surrender our status, claims, rights, and reputations for the good of others.

The motive for our love for and service to others is the knowledge that we are loved by God. This is a crucial point because it could seem that humility is simply thinking that everyone else is better than you and that you're not worth much. But humility does not consist in hanging your head or having a miserable opinion of yourself. That can seem humble because you appear to have a low opinion of yourself. But because this low opinion is filled with shame and regret, it is not true humility.

Arrogance and despair turn out to be two sides of the same coin. One is an inflated view of oneself; the other is a deflated view (the balloon has been pricked). But pride and self-pity share an excessive concern about oneself.

Excessive concern about oneself cannot give rise to genuine love for others. False humility won't take risks in caring for others. It may be nice, but it is not loving. It may listen attentively, but it must stop short of challenging, hard words because false humility depends too heavily on others' opinions.

True humility, confident in Christ's love, can show genuine love, can be willing to lay down the other's good thoughts about you for the sake of helping them. You can move toward prickly people, even if they are coming against you, because you know that Christ moved toward you in love, while you were yet his enemy. Humility sets you free from self-concern to focus on and care for others.

> *Exercise:* Make yourself available to others. Move toward someone you find difficult or someone you find yourself withdrawing from.

Ask God to show you where you can serve them: your house, your neighborhood, work, and church.

5. Humility is a joyful response to reality beyond ourselves.

How can you escape from the prison of pride to the freedom of true humility? Simply trying to become humble is like trying to escape from quicksand: the more you struggle to get free, the deeper you sink.

While we must be on guard, vigilant against pride in ourselves, you can't develop humility by looking at yourself and trying to catch yourself in the act of being proud—or of being humble, for that matter. What actually helps us gain a truly humble self-estimation is to encounter reality beyond ourselves.

A simple example of this is when you're engaged in activities that take you out of yourself. For Brian this comes in moments of teaching, playing guitar, and playing basketball. It happens when he is immersed in the game, especially when he's in "the zone," rather than reflecting on himself in relation to the game. The same is true when you're watching a game and your team makes an amazing shot: you stand up and cheer without thinking about it. Likewise, with skillful activities, you are taken out of yourself and into what Matthew Crawford calls "the world beyond your head."[22]

Existential philosophers describe this with the Greek word *ekstasis*. Our word *ecstasy* comes from this word, and it literally means "standing outside" oneself. When we retreat into ourselves, we lose confidence and the ability to trust. Think of Peter walking on the water. While he was looking at Jesus with full trust, he was able to walk on water. But when he looked at himself standing on the water, he began to sink (Matt. 14:28–30).

We humans tend to relate everything back to ourselves, but humility takes us out of ourselves. It allows us to delight in the goodness, truth, and beauty of persons and things "for [their] own sake."[23] This is particularly challenging in the age of selfies and social media, when every experience and encounter is possible material for our online profiles. Everything has value in terms of our curated online selves.

Humility recognizes that things have great value independent of me and my will. Humility smiles. It laughs. It worships. It comes when we know ourselves in relation to that which transcends us.

We see this throughout the Bible—people confidently making their way through a world that is familiar and comfortable ... until they encounter some manifestation of God: a burning bush, a vision of God's glory, or sometimes an angel. When this happens, the human response is always a profound (and accurate!) sense of unworthiness (Luke 5:8). They did not reach this realization by reflecting on themselves. What humbled them was an encounter with the holiness and glory of God (Isa. 6:5).

Encountering the glory of God brings us to our knees (Rev. 1:17). This glory takes us out of ourselves and draws us into worship as we see that praise and thanksgiving are the only fitting responses to the wonder of God (4:10–11). Sensing God's glory allows us to transcend ourselves, displacing us from the center of our reality.

We also experience this self-transcendence when we wonder at the created world. This is one way nature restores us—when we consider the glories of creation—infinitely vast and infinitely small, endlessly diverse in its varieties of animals and plants.

We also experience self-transcendence in the mysteries of life: when we truly encounter another person—not as an obstacle or a means but as a *person*—we meet the image of God in the world. In that moment when you first hold your newborn child in your arms, you are not thinking about yourself. There is now another person, another perspective in the world.

We can experience this with our friends and families as well as with our enemies and those we might prefer to ignore: the widow, the orphan, the stranger, the poor, the sick, embarrassing relatives, and obnoxious neighbors. We *see* them. Humility finds the beauty of God's love in unlikely places. A cruciform imagination allows us to see with the eyes of Christ, in some small way to see other people as God sees them (2 Cor. 5:16).

Humility takes an interest in the good, the true, and the beautiful for their own sake. All of this stands in contrast to pride, which is blind to these humble manifestations of God's glory. And when pride does perceive glory in other persons and things, it resents that glory as a threat to its own.[24] For pride seeks its own glory and is hostile to all rivals.

The way out of this pride is the way of the cross, which is dying to ourselves and the quest for our glory. Humility means being displaced so that we no longer see ourselves as the center of reality. But we cannot be displaced unless something or someone replaces us. This is why the way to humility is not to focus on self and try to determine whether we are humble or not. Rather, it is the practice of becoming increasingly attuned to all the glory, goodness, truth, and beauty beyond ourselves. That is the surest way to lose ourselves—and paradoxically, to know ourselves.

> *Exercise:* Spend time in worship. This is the best, truest way to be taken out of yourself. Learn to worship God in a variety of places, first and foremost with the church but also by delighting in his glory throughout your daily life.

6. Humility means becoming like a little child.

One of Jesus' most famous statements on humility came in response to his disciples' question, "Who is the greatest in the kingdom of heaven?" (Matt. 18:1). Jesus responded by calling a child to him and saying, "Truly, I say to you, unless you turn and become like children, you will never enter the kingdom of heaven. Whoever humbles himself like this child is the greatest in the kingdom of heaven" (vv. 3–4).

Like many of Jesus' teachings, this one is a bit perplexing. What does it mean to become like a child?

Children are remarkable because they delight in things for their own sake. There's an immediacy to their interest in things. This can make it difficult for them to do things that require long-term planning and delayed gratification—practicing the piano, for instance—and part of maturity is growing out of this. But this maturity brings its own danger: namely, that of seeing everything in terms of how it affects us.

This is what we see with most of the adults who interacted with Jesus: they were trying to assess who he was and what he meant for their religious programs and projects. How did he affect them? How did Jesus fit into their plans? How did he satisfy their ambitions and fulfill their expectations? The children who encountered Jesus approached him with a simple delight in who he was. They were drawn simply to his goodness and love. They wanted to be with Jesus (Mark 10:16).

Consider the story of the rich young ruler who approached Jesus and asked, "Good Teacher, what must I do to inherit eternal life?" (Luke 18:18). The ruler was a lot like many affluent late-modern westerners: he was already living out his vision of the good life. He was rich, he was young, and he had political power. And like many of us, he thought of himself as a "good person."

Jesus directed him to the law, and the ruler reported that he hadn't committed adultery, murdered, stolen, or lied, and he had honored his parents. He would make an ideal son-in-law. He just needed one last element to top off his good life: to know how to inherit eternal life. Jesus saw this and told him, "Sell all that you have and distribute to the poor, and you will have treasure in heaven; and come, follow me" (v. 22).

As usual, Jesus went right to the heart of the matter. The rich young ruler was not looking for his entire life to be oriented around Jesus. He was just looking to add one last religious ingredient to top off what was already a pretty good life. He didn't want that life to be turned upside down. Like many of us, he was looking for a bit of religion to reach that last level on Maslow's famous hierarchy of needs: self-actualization. We don't want that hierarchy to be overturned either. The question is, do we want just a bit of religion to add an overlay of meaning and purpose to an otherwise good life? Or do we want *Jesus*?

Along with children, the other people who delighted in Jesus for his own sake were those who had no illusions that they were living the good life: sinners, prostitutes, and tax collectors. And when he called them out of their sin to come follow him, perhaps they did so because they knew that there is no true life apart from him. Humility grounds us in reality.

> *Exercise:* Ask yourself, "What am I carrying that a little child would not? What am I carrying that the rich young ruler did? Do I really want Jesus, or am I just looking for some happy, inspirational thoughts that won't overturn the balance in my life?"

7. Humility delights in excellence.

We often imagine that humility means having no drive or ambition and settling for uninspired, mediocre work. We need to reimagine humility in its fullest sense, because it is most definitely not an excuse for mediocrity. As we saw in the last chapter, humility delights in excellence.

Humility responds to what is good, true, and beautiful in any endeavor. This is true of our creative activities and athletic competitions. It is true for performances in music and dance, and it is true for our work. This is why we speak approvingly of people who "take pride in their work," by which we mean not pride in the sinful sense but a personal investment in doing things well.

Certainly the pursuit of excellence *can* go astray and become pride in the sinful sense, but when it is rightly ordered, it is a good thing. It's always a temptation to seek our own glory through our work, for our hearts to be lifted or deflated based on how our work is received. This is true for pastors in their pulpits and professors at their lecterns. It's true for authors. It's true for everyone. We're all prone to find our self-worth in our work and therefore to tie our hearts to the results, to be inflated by accomplishment or deflated by criticism.

One maxim you can place over all your work is "Master, I'm here to do your bidding." Then you can release the results of your work to God. You can do your work with all your heart while also loving the Lord your God with all your heart. An actor before she walks into an audition can say, "Master, I'm here to do your bidding." An elementary-school teacher can say it before he begins a class, as can a doctor before a surgery. Doing your job to please God is a way to stitch humility into a realm that often squeezes humility out—our daily work.

Jesus never prohibits his followers from pursuing greatness. He says humility is what greatness looks like to him. He doesn't seem embarrassed about our desire to be rewarded or our aspiration to be considered great. He just redefines greatness. He says this is the *kind* of greatness he wants us to pursue: learn to be a servant of all (Matt. 20:26).

For Jesus our greatness can be measured by our humility. And humility delights in greatness—not as a means of self-glorification but in service to others. Humility aspires to do excellent work, that it might be a blessing to others, that it might be life-giving. And in those times when our work turns out as somewhat less than we'd hoped, humility accepts that with joy as well.

> *Exercise:* Contemplate the created world—whether in the natural world or in human activities in art, science, and culture. Ask yourself, *What in this is good, true, and beautiful? What shows me the world as God has created it to be? What shows me the truth about human beings—as we are and as we were created to be?* Cultivate this in your own work and celebrate it in the work of others.

Finally, the most important exercise for the cultivation of humility is to simply ask God for it. He will answer your prayer. He delights to grant the prayer of the one who asks for the very thing he wishes to give (1 John 5:14–15).

CRUCIFORM
FREEDOM

In 1962 the Swiss theologian Karl Barth made his one and only American tour. This was a momentous event for American readers of Barth. It was also an opportunity for Barth to practice his English (which he had learned mostly from reading detective novels). During a panel discussion at the University of Chicago, Barth spoke about what kind of theology he would write if he were American: "I would try to elaborate a theology of freedom"— especially "that freedom to which the Son frees us ... which as his gift, is the one real human freedom."[1]

"The one real human freedom." Barth's phrase implies that there are *false* ideas of freedom out there and that sorting out the difference between true and false freedom is a vital task for followers of Jesus.

Freedom is one of the classic philosophical questions, one that comes up in an Intro to Philosophy course: Do we have free will, or are our choices determined for us? But the nature of freedom is not a topic for only college students, philosophers, and theologians. It is a key question for each of us in the modern world since freedom is so central to our understanding of ourselves and what makes for a healthy society.

This is especially true in the United States, which was founded on the idea of "Life, Liberty and the pursuit of Happiness." The Declaration of Independence names these as "unalienable Rights" given equally to all human beings by God. A big part of American history is the willingness to fight to attain this freedom and to preserve it. That's why we hear phrases like "Liberty or death." Or as the license plate of New Hampshire says it, "Live Free or Die."

The idea of freedom is part of the *grandeur* and the *misère* of American culture, to borrow a phrase from Blaise Pascal.[2] This idea is one of America's greatest strengths as well as one of its greatest weaknesses. It brings a spirit of seemingly endless possibilities and, with it, seemingly endless temptations to misunderstand or misuse our freedom.

In his classic book *Democracy in America,* Alexis de Tocqueville observes that one of the dangers in a democracy like America's is that its individualism can create a false sense of independence, such that we start to think we "owe nothing to anyone"—neither our ancestors, our descendants, nor our contemporaries. This narrowing vision leads the democratic man "back toward himself alone and threatens finally to confine him wholly in the solitude of his own heart." In the end, "each citizen is habitually occupied in contemplating a very small object, which is himself."[3]

Certainly this temptation afflicts American Christianity. The church has benefited enormously from the religious freedoms of the United States, but a false form of freedom can quickly become an idol. The false freedom of American Christianity can take the shape of individualistic forms of faith that revolve around the self, fulfilling its own needs and desires and catering to its particular preferences. The self is beholden to no tradition or authority, no external limits. A person pursuing this false freedom might say, "I am free to choose the religious beliefs and practices that work for me." As Ross Douthat observes, we have become a nation of heretics.[4] *Hairesis*, the Greek word from which we get *heresy*, actually means "choice."[5]

The main reason Christians must reject this individualistic view of freedom is that it is completely unbiblical. Nowhere in the Bible does freedom mean radical individualism. For Jesus, that is a recipe for slavery (John 8:34; Rom. 6:16). Biblical freedom is always relational and tied to love—love of God and love of others.

We have said that God's wisdom for the good, beautiful life is the cruciform life, and the cruciform life means that everything must now be reinterpreted in light of the cross. This includes our view of freedom. What does freedom mean in light of the cross?

In this chapter we will contrast false ideas of freedom with the one true freedom we find in the Christian story.

It turns out that true freedom takes the shape of the cross. True freedom comes not through breaking away from all constraints but by living according to the true order of things. True freedom comes not through seeking our own agendas but through denying ourselves and following after Jesus' will. The cross frees us from that which binds us—namely, ourselves. True freedom comes not through our projects of self-making but through losing ourselves. True freedom does not exalt or promote self-interests but seeks to serve others in love. Only this cruciform freedom leads to genuine human flourishing.

PORTRAITS OF (FALSE) FREEDOM

What is freedom? Many people would define it as this: "Freedom is being able to do what you want." That's a good starting point, but it needs clarification. What does it mean to be able to do what you want? This is where things quickly get more complicated. A lot of the time, this notion of *doing what you want* can smuggle into thinking false ideas about freedom.

Consider the following portraits of false freedom:

1. *The Romantic Self.* According to this narrative, which came out of a philosophy called Romanticism, we humans are at our most free when we are on our own, prior to society. We are naturally free, but society constrains us. In philosopher Jean-Jacques Rousseau's words, "Man is born free, and everywhere he is in chains."[6]

2. *The Bachelor/Bachelorette.* This vision says we are free when we are not tied down by commitments and obligations. Of

romantic relationships, this kind of freedom asks: Why would I want to tie myself down to one person—the proverbial ball and chain? Why limit my options? An extreme version is the figure of Don Juan (or in today's terms, the *player*), for whom an open field of romantic possibilities is much more interesting than the actuality of marriage, which is considered boring and bourgeois.

3. *The Devil.* Modern culture has come to think of the Devil as a figure of freedom—a tragic hero who stood up against a tyrannical God. As Satan says in John Milton's *Paradise Lost,* "Better to reign in Hell, than serve in Heaven."[7] A more recent version of this figure appears in the movie *The Devil's Advocate,* with Al Pacino (playing the Devil) giving a monologue that makes his case against God.[8] In his argument, God created a world filled with sensual pleasures and then set the rules against us by forbidding everything he created. The path of freedom, then, is to see through these arbitrary rules and live a life of indulgence.

4. *The Disney Princess.* In the movie *Frozen,* Princess Elsa has a secret power: she can wield ice. She has hidden this power her whole life to protect the people in her kingdom. But in the solitude of the mountains, she is finally able to unleash her power and be her true self, with no restraints. She sings, "It's time to see what I can do, to test the limits and break through! No right, no wrong, no rules for me, I'm free!"[9] Mermaid Ariel longs to leave the confines of the ocean; Belle longs to abandon her provincial life; Rapunzel longs to escape her tower prison; Cinderella longs to get away from the influence of her wicked

stepmother. Each of these heroines must break free from the restraints of her story in order to truly live, according to the Disney story line.

5. *Iron Man or the Transhumanist.* Thanks to science and technology, we are increasingly liberated from the constraints and demands of our natural physical existence. Thus, we see some transhumanists who aspire to upload their consciousness and achieve immortality by leaving behind their bodies entirely, thus achieving a sort of freedom.

6. *The Tyrant.* In antiquity the figure of the tyrant was attractive insofar as he seemed to be the freest member of his realm. Subject to no one, he held absolute power. His wish was everyone else's command. The idea of the tyrant appealed to people who wanted to rule with absolute power. Nowadays most people don't wish to be tyrants (or wouldn't use that term, even if that's what they desire). Maintaining tyrannical rule demands constant cunning and intrigue, since tyrants never know whom they can trust. For most of us this seems like more trouble than it's worth. Who needs the hassle?

7. *The Rich, Financially Independent Person Living a Comfortable Life.* Consider the song "I'm Free" by the Rolling Stones. In 1965 Mick Jagger sings, "I'm free to do what I want any old time."[10] Like other cultural artifacts of the sixties, that freewheeling spirit has now been coopted by the marketplace. Chase Bank used the song in an ad for their Freedom credit card line, and the auto company Renault used it in an ad for a new SUV. The implication is clear: freedom equals money and

cars. And what money and cars have in common is that they promise to extricate us from the things that bind so we are free to do what we want.

TRUE FREEDOM NEEDS LIMITS

These portraits are all recognizable in our society today, from films and songs to advertising and political speeches. There are problems, however, with each of these images of freedom.

What they all have in common is that they conceive of freedom only in *negative* terms. They define freedom as the absence of constraint, obstacle, or interference. I am free when nothing is stopping me from doing what I want. I am free *from* other people, from society and government, from tradition and authority, from nature and my body, and maybe even from God.

Freedom means breaking the limits. No rules, no boundaries. No one tells me what to do. I decide for myself. I'm free. We bristle at rules, laws, and boundaries because they seem to be the opposite of freedom. This kind of freedom means refusing to live by the rules or prescriptions of anyone else.

But this popular view of freedom is naive and quickly falls apart under any sort of pressure.

A terrific challenge to this idea is *The LEGO Movie*.[11] Emmet Brickowski lives in the LEGO city of Bricksburg, which operates entirely according to instruction manuals. He seems happy, singing "everything is awesome," but only because he is wearing a generic happy face and is unaware of any other way of life.

One day, however, he meets a cool rebel girl named Wyldstyle and finds himself drawn into the resistance against an evil dictator named Lord Business, who enforces the by-the-book lifestyle of Bricksburg.

Emmet is hiding an uncomfortable secret: he is the victim of a case of mistaken identity. Wyldstyle thinks he is a Master Builder like her, but he is not. Master Builders are not bound by instruction manuals. They use their imaginations to come up with their own original LEGO creations. Emmet has never done anything original in his life. In the end, though, he learns to be creative, and the movie culminates in a grand confrontation in which all the residents of Bricksburg throw off the shackles of their instruction manuals and use their bricks to create new things to fight against Lord Business and his oppressive forces.

At first glance this might seem to be the same old message: freedom and creativity versus rules and control. But *The LEGO Movie* is more subtle (and subversive) than that. Master Builders don't create without *any* sense of rules or boundaries. That sort of completely freeform creation is what happens in Cloud Cuckoo Land, where there are no rules and everything is, well, *cuckoo*. But even the chaos of Cloud Cuckoo Land depends on some basic sense of how LEGOs work.

LEGO pieces cannot be put together in a truly random way. They interconnect according to a strict internal logic. This system offers a vast field of possibilities. It gives enormous freedom to create new things, to build in new ways. Imagination is essential. But everyone who has ever played with LEGOs also knows that if you don't build things according to this logic, they don't work. Towers collapse. One wall is shorter than another. Pieces don't overlap. Things fall apart. The center cannot hold. Mere anarchy is loosed upon the world ... or something like that.

Instead of overthrowing all rules, Master Builders create within the constraints of the LEGO system. Their freedom is a union of possibilities that open and constraints that close: freedom *within boundaries is the LEGO way.*

In this regard, LEGOs are very much like real life. We are free, imaginative creatures who create new things. We are subcreators. Our creative activity is an expression of our having been made in the image of the creator God. At the same time, our creativity and freedom are always limited by real constraints. There is no such thing as freedom without some limits. There are the basic limits of nature: I'm not free to live underwater like a fish or fly off buildings like a bird. We are not free to ignore the law of gravity. If my freedom means ignoring gravity, I will quickly find myself unable to act freely at all. Freedom must respect the laws of nature.

There are also the limits that come with living with other people: I'm not free to borrow a fire truck to drive my kids to school, and I'm not free to interpret red lights as green. Doing these things will quickly mean the end of my freedom.

Often people will say that freedom means being able to do what I want, provided I don't physically hurt anyone else. This understanding of freedom has been enshrined in law by the Supreme Court: "At the heart of liberty is the right to define one's own concept of existence, of meaning, of the universe."[12] We are free to come up with whatever meaning of the universe we prefer. The question, though, is whether the universe is obligated to play along.

There are laws of nature, and there are human laws. Both put limits on freedom. But even more fundamentally, there is what Saint Augustine calls the *eternal* law. This is the law of moral and spiritual reality. The eternal law is the standard by which things may be rightly or justly ordered.[13] The eternal law has to do with the kind of creatures that we are—what it is for us to be rightly ordered and what it is to flourish as the kind of beings we are. This law is written into the very fabric of creation, and it is no more flexible than the laws of physics, chemistry, or biology. To ignore it is to court disaster—no less so than to ignore the law of gravity. Break the eternal law, and you break your life.

For Augustine human freedom is possible only when we follow the eternal law. As he writes, "The only genuine freedom is that possessed by those who are happy and cleave to the eternal law."[14]

Notice what Augustine is saying: *only the happy are free.* And who are the happy? They are those who cleave to the eternal law. The eternal law shows us what it is to be rightly ordered—our hearts and minds, our desires and affections. When our souls are rightly ordered, then we are at last free to do what we want. But therein lies the question of freedom: What do we want?

WHAT DO YOU WANT?

If we define freedom solely in negative terms—as freedom *from* interference or obstacles—it is still not clear what freedom is *for*.

It doesn't really help to answer, "You are free for whatever you want to be free for." Supposing I'm free to do what I want "any old time," as Mick Jagger sings, the big question is still, *What do I want?* That seemingly obvious question is in fact quite difficult to answer.

How do I know what I *really* want? I might suppose that my strongest desire is what I really want. But that approach doesn't work, because we often have conflicts between what we want right now and what we want in the long term. I want to sleep in, but I also want to keep my job. I want seconds (and maybe thirds) on dessert, but I also want to be fit and healthy.

Taking what I want in the moment may feel like freedom, but I need, at minimum, impulse control and the ability to delay gratification if I am going to pursue long-term goals and more significant desires. Indulging in immediate desires has a way of quickly making us unfree. As Augustine puts it, we end up serving the things that are meant to serve us.[15] Instead of using material things, I become attached to them. Instead of enjoying food to nourish my body, I eat when I know I shouldn't. Instead of having a drink to relax or celebrate, I become preoccupied with when I can get another drink. I do what I don't want and don't do what I want (Rom. 7:19).

This is where we can benefit by looking back to see the premodern idea of freedom.

In the ancient world, Greek philosophy and Christianity agreed that freedom meant following my desires and doing what I want, but everything depended on my desires being rightly ordered. I am free when my desires are directed toward the good. I am free when my will is formed by virtue so that I want what is truly good for me, not just what appears good in the moment. This is why we can't understand freedom in merely negative terms. Freedom can't be defined solely as what I am free *from*. Real freedom also involves a clear sense of what I am free *for*.

To be free, we must ask: What are we made for?

Augustine's answer to this question is a famous one, but it has lost none of its brilliance though quoted in a million sermons. In the beginning of his *Confessions*, he addresses God: "To praise you is the desire of man, a little piece of your creation. You stir man to take pleasure in praising you, because you have made us for yourself, and our heart is restless until it rests in you."[16]

God has created us to know, love, and worship him. As the Westminster Shorter Catechism puts it, our purpose is "to glorify God, and to enjoy him forever."[17] What are we made for? We are created for *communion with God*. Our desires are rightly ordered when we seek first our enjoyment in God (Matt. 6:33). This is genuine human freedom and flourishing.

WHOM THE SON SETS FREE IS FREE INDEED

Our problem is that we tend to seek our joy in the wrong things. This is the simplest definition of sin. We refuse to believe that God wants our deepest happiness, so instead of obeying God, we seek happiness on our own terms or by our own understanding. But

Jesus says in order to be free in the way we were made to be—free for God—we need to be set free from sin. And, as it turns out, it is not so easy for our desires to be rightly ordered. It's not as simple as just deciding to want the good. Our condition is one of radical *un*freedom. This is a consequence of sin.

There is a long-standing narrative that sin is the path of freedom. The enemy of our freedom, we are told, is a god who wants to control or limit us with his commandments (Gen. 3:4–5). We think freedom is the ability to choose for ourselves how to live. This is the story we like to tell ourselves, but Jesus tells a different story. In John 8:34 Jesus says, "Everyone who practices sin is a slave to sin." Sin pretends to be freedom, but what starts as freedom quickly turns into unfreedom.

We were created to live freely before God and to inhabit his world as free creatures—partaking of created goods but never treating them as if they are our true source of life. Only when we are in right relation to God are we truly free. We are free in relation to other people, we are free in relation to created things, and we are free in relation to ourselves.

But when we turn away from God, our center of gravity changes. We turn to ourselves and seek to enjoy ourselves and God's creation by ourselves. God becomes a threat to our self-enclosed enjoyment. And to recall Augustine's words, we end up serving the things that are meant to serve us.

As we mentioned in chapter 2, this is the condition that thinkers like Augustine, Bernard of Clairvaux, and Martin Luther have described as "incurvature." When the human heart curves in on itself, we make our wills—ourselves—the center of all reality. This is one sense in which the Bible uses the term *the flesh* (*sarx*). The flesh is not the material, physical body per se but an existential orientation of being curved in on oneself in sin.

In his sermon "Kingship," George MacDonald describes the lie that resides at the heart of incurvature: "I am my own king and my own subject.... My own glory is, and ought to be, my chief care.... My pleasure is my pleasure.... I will be free with the freedom that consists in doing whatever I am inclined to do.... To do my own will so long as I feel anything to be my will, is to be free, is to live."[18]

Incurvature operates with a false picture of the self, a false picture of life, and a false picture of freedom. The self imagines it is its own sovereign lord and master, its own king.

This is precisely what Jesus challenges. Jesus entered the world, proclaiming himself as the true king. But he is a king who does not oppress his people.

In the same sermon MacDonald continues, "Jesus is a king because his business is to bear witness to the truth. What truth? All truth; all verity of relation throughout the universe—first of all, that his father is good, perfectly good; and that the crown and joy of life is to desire and do the will of the eternal source of will, and of all life. He deals thus the death-blow to the power of hell."[19]

And what is the power of hell? According to MacDonald, hell runs according to one principle: "I am my own."[20] This is the very principle that underlies so much of our false idea of freedom and autonomy and those portraits we looked at earlier. *I am my own.* I am my own creator. I am my own master and king. One of my (Brian's) students puts this in a particularly memorable way: "Hands off, God!" Yet this is what Jesus confronts:

> Jesus said to the Jews who had believed him, "If you abide in my word, you are truly my disciples, and you will know the truth, and the truth will set you free." They answered him, "We are offspring of Abraham and have never been enslaved to anyone. How is it that you say, 'You will become free'?"
>
> Jesus answered them, "Truly, truly, I say to you, everyone who practices sin is a slave to sin. The slave does not remain in the house forever; the son remains forever. So if the Son sets you free, you will be free indeed. I know that you are offspring of Abraham; yet you seek to kill me because my word finds no place in you. I speak of what I have seen with my Father, and you do what you have heard from your father." (John 8:31–38)

"The truth will set you free." You've probably heard that saying quoted many times. It is often cited to suggest that knowing the truth means having the right ideas in your mind. If you can just access the right information, you will be free. But ideas and information alone do not set us free.

Jesus was saying that he is the truth in person, in flesh. Jesus is the truth, and it is Jesus who sets us free from the power of sin. Whom the Son sets free is free indeed.

The confrontation here is as fundamental as it gets: Who is the true king? Who is lord of your life? If it is Jesus, we will become free, as we were made to be (Eph. 4:24). If we insist on being our own masters, then our freedom is actually the greatest bondage. Why? Because the self is such a tremendous burden to bear.

In "Who Shall Deliver Me?" the great nineteenth-century poet Christina Rossetti expresses this burden beautifully:

> God strengthen me to bear myself;
> That heaviest weight of all to bear,
> Inalienable weight of care …
>
> Myself, arch-traitor to myself;
> My hollowest friend, my deadliest foe,
> My clog whatever road I go.
>
> Yet One there is can curb myself,
> Can roll the strangling load from me,
> Break off the yoke and set me free.[21]

The problem with the popular advice "Just be yourself!" is that the incurved self is stuck with itself. As Pascal observes, "Self-will will never be satisfied, though it should have command of all it would; but we are satisfied from the moment we renounce it."[22]

As we've seen, there is a proper self-esteem and self-love that come with being a creature of God: the recognition that God made us. There is a dignity to our being and our activities that should be recognized. But we were not created to soak in fascination with self. We were made to transcend ourselves, to look not in the mirror but through windows, so we can regard the world outside ourselves: God's creatures and ultimately God himself. We are relational beings created for communion with God and others. True freedom is relational and always includes love.

But how do we make this happen? How do we open ourselves to God and others? Jesus' point is that we can't! The self cannot set itself free! We need God to set us free, free from the heaviest weight of all to bear: ourselves. Every attempt to liberate ourselves from our own captivity just leads into another cell in the prison of incurvature. We try to make ourselves better, but our attempts at self-making still follow the basic logic of self-justification. Our understanding of freedom needs to be reinterpreted in light of the cross. True freedom is cruciform freedom.

CHRIST SET US FREE FOR FREEDOM

The French existentialist philosopher Jean-Paul Sartre famously writes that "man is nothing else but what he makes of himself."[23] Sartre presents this as a state of exhilarating freedom: I am entirely responsible for myself. Yet Sartre also recognizes that this freedom is a state of immense anxiety. There is no grace, only responsibility. I am never free in relation to others because I must justify my existence at every turn.

The cross presents us with a radically different understanding of existence—one governed by the logic of God's gift. We were set free in relation to God. Our communion with God is based not on our performance but on an unconditional gift.[24] If we insist that we need to add something to Christ, to God's gift, that we must supplement it or earn it in some fashion, then we still don't understand the nature of the gift. We are made free because this communion is unconditional. When a relationship is conditional, when it depends on our performance, we are not really free. This is why Paul writes, "It was for freedom that Christ set us free" (Gal. 5:1 NASB).

The Bible makes a puzzling claim: Christ has set us free for freedom. It might sound a bit negative or circular: freedom is being free for … *freedom*? It's not immediately clear what the content of that freedom might be.

What is at stake in Paul's letter to the Galatians is the question of justification (i.e., how one becomes just, or righteous, before God). Sin means things are not right between us and God. How is our situation rectified? How are we made right? On what basis can we stand before God, enter into relation with God, and be in communion with God? Paul recognizes only two possibilities: we are made right either by observing the law or by having faith in Christ. Paul's answer is clear: "By works of the law no one will be justified" (2:16). It is only by faith in Christ that we are justified.

This is a simple truth, yet it is eminently difficult to grasp. We are justified by faith, not by works. We need to be reminded of this constantly because we always tend to resort to some kind of strategy of trying to justify our own lives. And most of the time, this is how the world works, especially in America: a logic of reciprocal exchange. You get what you deserve, what you earn, and what you pay for.

The temptation for all Christians is to suppose that we need Jesus ... plus something else. We get a good start with salvation, but then (the thinking goes) we had better add some program, some practical extension, or something else to make ourselves worthy of what Jesus has given. It may be some kind of spiritual discipline, special knowledge or learning, work of service, or spiritual experience.

But this is theology of glory, not the way of the cross. When we slip into this mode of thinking, we are no longer trusting that the gift of God's grace is sufficient. We fall back into the logic of self-justification. Even our best moral and religious efforts, when not done in faith, are works of the flesh because they are not done out of trust in Christ, who alone makes us righteous. It's so easy for us to fall back into the slavery of trying to justify ourselves (Rom. 8:14–17).

Only when we act in faith, trusting in the gift of God in Christ alone, are we truly free. Then our actions are not motivated by a need to justify ourselves. We are already justified by faith. Because of the cross, we are in Christ. And because we are in Christ, we no longer act because we have to but out of the overflow of God's love. Because we are in Christ, we are set free for others—to serve others in love. Only in Christ are we free. But to the extent that we try to supplement the work of Christ, to that extent we have fallen from grace (Gal. 5:4) and are falling back into the slavery we have been set free from.

Part of what makes sin so sad is that we prefer our familiar prisons. The door is locked from the inside.

FREEDOM FOR OTHERS

It may sound strange to say that we are set free for service, but it's true. Freedom and service seem like opposites, yet this is the freedom that Christianity offers. The incurved self sees freedom as *self*-serving, which of course affects how we see others.

There are only three ways for the incurved self to view other people: (1) they are part of my own enjoyment of life (so I manipulate); (2) they are obstacles in the way of my enjoyment (so I get angry); and (3) as long as they don't interfere with me, they should be free to pursue whatever it is that makes them happy (so I'm indifferent).

As we have seen, the problem with incurvature is that it imagines freedom to be directed toward the self: I am free to do what I want (i.e., to serve myself). The cross shows us a freedom that is not self-seeking but is directed outward, toward others.

Cruciform freedom is self-denying and self-sacrificial. It does not insist on its own rights. Jesus did not insist that everyone recognize his true status as the Son of God. Instead, he showed us the true heart of God—a love that gives itself for others. That is the heart of true freedom. Hence Martin Luther's famous statement: "A

Christian is a perfectly free lord of all, subject to none. A Christian is a perfectly dutiful servant of all, subject to all."[25]

We are set free for something—to serve something more than ourselves. And we can truly serve because we are free. This service is not a task we must perform to earn something or get something. Freely we have received, so freely we give. Kierkegaard describes this service as "works of love," but these works are not works aimed at earning God's favor. They are works in response to God's grace and love—"a striving born of gratitude."[26]

Does loving others without conditions sound appealing? Does this sound like real freedom and the good life? Maybe for a few high-minded idealists, but those of us who are less noble might still be thinking, *Yuck*. Too often we think about service, about works of love, as though they are the broccoli of life— good for our health but maybe not all that enjoyable. Although Kierkegaard says our works of love are motivated by gratitude, it still might seem as if we are just gritting our teeth and doing things we would rather not do. Kierkegaard's point, however, is that this love is an overflowing of God's love for us. The source of this love is hidden. Here's how he describes "love's hidden life": "Just as the quiet lake originates deep down in hidden springs no eye has seen, so also does a person's love originate even more deeply in God's love. If there were no gushing spring at the bottom, if God were not love, then there would be neither the little lake nor a human being's love. Just as the quiet lake originates darkly in the deep spring, so a human being's love originates mysteriously in God's love."[27]

So we love those around us—not because we have to but out of the overflow of God's love. Our imaginations are transformed so that we begin to see others as God sees them, because of how God loves us (1 John 4:19).

We began chapter 1 with this statement: "We all want to be happy." It's true. We all want to enjoy rich, meaningful lives. But Jesus tells us that those who seek their own lives will lose them (Luke 9:24). If we focus all our attention and energy on getting the most out of our own lives, the scope of those lives will narrow rather than expand; they will shrivel rather than flourish. It is only in losing our lives that we find them. That is the wisdom of the way of the cross.

The deeper we live into this wisdom, the more we participate in the life-giving love of God. The deeper our participation in this love, the more our desires are reordered so that we are living in accord with the deepest reality of the universe. Then we will be living as the creatures we were created to be. That is the "one real human freedom"[28] and the path of true human flourishing.

———————

One of the most beloved scenes in Victor Hugo's novel *Les Misérables* is the redemption of Jean Valjean.

Valjean is a convict recently released from prison. He is free, but he isn't really free. He has nowhere to sleep, so he finds shelter in the home of a local bishop. Valjean repays this hospitality by stealing the bishop's silverware in the night. Valjean may have been set free from prison, but he isn't free from the need to steal or his own hardness of heart.

Valjean is quickly caught and taken back to the bishop in the police's custody. His brief moment of freedom has quickly turned, and he expects he will return to prison. Valjean is therefore stunned when the bishop brings no charges against him. Instead, the bishop hands him silver candlesticks, pretending it had all been a gift and Valjean had merely forgotten to take them along with the rest of the silver. The bishop dismisses the police, and Valjean is dumbfounded.

Up to this moment, Valjean has not been free. He had been freed from prison, but he wasn't free not to steal. Valjean was doubly constrained. First, he was an ex-convict with no money, no prospects, no place to go. Socially, he was trapped. But he was also trapped spiritually. He couldn't help but repay the bishop's hospitality by stealing from him.

The bishop addresses both of Valjean's constraints. His response is not purely spiritual, like the person in the epistle of James: "If a brother or sister is poorly clothed and lacking in daily food, and one of you says to them, 'Go in peace, be warmed and filled,' without giving them the things needed for the body, what good is that?" (James 2:15–16). The bishop's silverware and candlesticks give Valjean the money he needs to start a new life.

The bishop also sets Valjean free spiritually. Valjean is redeemed, ransomed, bought with a price: "Jean Valjean, my brother: you belong no longer to evil, but to good. It is your soul that I am buying for you. I withdraw it from dark thoughts and from the spirit of perdition, and I give it to God!"[29]

With this sublime act of mercy, the bishop sets Valjean free. He pronounces a word of grace that opens a new future before Valjean. He is set free for God, for good, to serve others. This is precisely what Valjean does, as he eventually becomes the benefactor to an entire town, and the redeemer and guardian of Cosette, a helpless orphan girl.

This is where Valjean finds his freedom—not in serving himself, but in serving others. And this is why Valjean has become one of the most beloved characters, not only in Hugo's novel but in all world literature. It is clear to everyone who reads this novel that Valjean is a picture of the good and beautiful life.

We may not have Victor Hugo to tell our stories. We have someone even better: the God who makes beautiful lives out of surrender.

CRUCIFORM LOVE

I believe that unarmed truth and unconditional love will have the final word in reality. This is why right temporarily defeated is stronger than evil triumphant.

Martin Luther King Jr., Nobel Peace Prize acceptance speech, 1964

Alain de Botton is a bestselling author who strives to show philosophy's relevance to everyday life. He dropped out of a PhD program at Harvard to write his first book, *Essays in Love*, which sold over two million copies. What launched him into even greater prominence was an article he wrote in 2016 published in the *New York Times*, entitled "Why You Will Marry the Wrong Person." The article opens, "It's one of the things we are most afraid might happen to us. We go to great lengths to avoid it. And yet we do it all the same: We marry the wrong person.... We seem normal only to those who don't know us very well. In a wiser, more self-aware society than our own, a standard question on any early dinner date would be: 'And how are you crazy?'"[1]

For de Botton, our problems in relationships usually stem from a lack of self-knowledge. We tend to think that *we* are not crazy and that we are not hard to live with, which leads us to place impossibly high expectations on one another.

De Botton claims further that we don't understand what love is. We have fallen prey to what he called "the Romantic view," that love is supposed to be instinctive ("You just know") or intuitive ("They just get me"), all the while not realizing that we are sabotaging our own relational prospects with these chronic misperceptions. We would be much better off, he counsels, if we reexamined not our lovers but our own view of love.

For de Botton, love is something we have to learn. We must grow in our ability to "tolerate differences with generosity" and demonstrate forgiveness and kindness to those we love. "Compatibility," de Botton concludes, "is an achievement of love; it must not be its precondition."[2]

On the list of most-read articles of 2016 in the *New York Times*, de Botton's "Why You Will Marry the Wrong Person" was number one. That is extraordinary when you recall that 2016 also included coverage of a presidential election, the Brexit vote, and the biggest refugee crisis of our era.

Evidently de Botton's thesis struck a chord. Why was it so popular? His own conjecture is that "we have an enormous loneliness around our difficulties,"[3] so it's consoling to have someone name what is so palpable for so many—disappointment in love.

"The good news," de Botton says, "is that it doesn't matter if we find we have married the wrong person. We mustn't abandon him or her, only the founding Romantic idea upon which the Western understanding of marriage has been based the last 250 years: that a perfect being exists who can meet all our needs and satisfy our every yearning."[4] As you might be able to glean from that last line, de Botton is an atheist. But whether or not you accept "that a perfect being exists who can meet all our needs," we can acknowledge that many of our relational difficulties revolve around our distorted view of love.

"Tell me the truth about love," the young W. H. Auden writes in one of his poems.[5] But we don't understand what true love entails.

LOVE IS A CROSS

The driving idea of this book is that the cross not only is the instrument of our salvation but also points us to a whole new way of being by establishing a new way of knowing—according to the cross. As we are fond of saying, everything must now be reinterpreted in light of the cross, including this slippery word *love*. The cross shows us what love is. "By this we know love, that he laid down his life for us" (1 John 3:16). Love is a cross.

When we encounter the love of God in Christ, it's wonderful beyond compare: "Amazing love! How can it be / That Thou, my God, shouldst die for me?"[6] But it can also be enormously traumatic. If dying (in any sense) for someone else is what love *means*, we must wonder, *Have I ever loved anyone in my life?* If the cross shows us what love is, we might ask, *Have I ever understood love before now?*

The twentieth-century theologian Hans Urs von Balthasar once wrote, "When man encounters the love of God in Christ, not only does he experience what genuine love is, but he is also confronted with the undeniable fact that he, a selfish sinner, does not himself possess true love.... Man cannot come to a recognition of [Jesus Christ] ... without a radical conversion—a conversion not only of the heart, which must in the face of this love confess that it has failed to love until now, but also a conversion of thought, which must *relearn* what love after all really is."[7]

God in Christ has revealed to the world what love is. Jesus was willing to lay down his life not simply for his friends, "but God shows his love for us in that while we were still sinners, Christ died for us" (Rom. 5:8). Before we agreed with him or even acknowledged him, indeed while we were yet his enemies, Christ laid down his life for us.

Love entails a self-sacrifice that is entirely undeserved. Love sets aside one's personal rights (Matt. 5:44–46). "[Love] does not insist on its own way" (1 Cor. 13:5). Nothing could stand further from our cultural moment's emphatic insistence on asserting your rights and preferences than this notion of setting aside your rights and sublimating your preferences for the sake of loving and serving another.

In our current polarized, politicized, tribal culture that is increasingly sorted along ideological lines and prone to dividing the world between "us and them," Jesus' model of love must, to borrow von Balthasar's words, lead to a radical conversion of the heart and thought.

Von Balthasar says that when you encounter the face of love in Christ, you are confronted with the undeniable fact that you have never loved anyone in your life. And we won't make any progress unless we confess that despite our deep desire to be loved, we may not ourselves know what it means to love.

When my wife and I (Rankin) became engaged, I rushed her to meet my grandparents, who were elderly and infirm. They had each played a significant role in my life, especially my grandfather, who was in his midnineties at the time. After I'd introduced my then fiancé to my grandparents, my grandfather announced that he'd like to take a drive out into the country and have a talk—just the two of us.

It was an undertaking. He had one of those foldable walkers— the kind with tennis balls on the feet—that he pushed in front of him. He positioned himself at the open passenger door and kind of just fell into the car, then asked me to help him swing his feet around and buckle his seat belt. I folded his walker and put it in the trunk, and we went for a drive.

Several minutes passed in silence until we found ourselves alone on an abandoned country road. Finally he broke the silence by asking, "Tell me, son—why do you want to marry this young woman?" I stammered but finally managed to get out, "There are a lot of reasons, but I guess the main one is that I love her."

At this he motioned with his right hand, pointing to the side of the road. That's old-man speak for "Pull the car over." So I pulled to the side of the road. Several more minutes passed in silence. I waited. Then he said, "Son, you don't know what love is." That's all he said. Then he motioned with his left hand. That's old-man speak for "You can get back on the road now." We drove home. And that's all he said. Thus ended the lesson.

It stung at the time. I had already been a pastor for a few years and thought I knew a little something. But I've lived to see the wisdom of his words. And all these years later, I count it among the most important things my grandfather ever said to me (Ps. 141:5).

My grandparents were married seventy years. Toward the end they had each lost control of basic bodily functions, but they tried, best as they could, to care for each other, washing each other, wiping the drool from one another's mouths.

I think they knew a little something about love.

BUT DO WE KNOW WHAT LOVE IS?

My grandfather had never heard of Hans Urs von Balthasar or Alain de Botton, but he was saying the same thing. And those three were saying what the apostle Paul was saying to his readers in Corinth two thousand years ago.

The believers in Corinth also thought they knew a little something. Like many in the ancient world, the citizens of Corinth placed a premium on knowledge (1 Cor. 8:1). They thought they were something because of their gifts. But Paul told them that if they hadn't learned what love is, it didn't matter how much they thought they knew or how much they'd gained. It all added up to nothing (13:2).

First Corinthians 13 is one of the most beloved chapters in the Bible. That's not surprising, but it's usually misunderstood. Taken out of context, it's one of the most beautiful and evocative treatments of love ever penned. In context, however, it might be one of the most terrifying chapters in Scripture.

Scholars tell us that in the ancient city of Corinth, citizens were very much concerned with their social status. They were obsessed with social climbing and distinguishing themselves. Not surprisingly, just like today, the values of the wider culture were infecting the church, creating all sorts of factions that were threatening to tear the young church apart.

Some had begun to think they were special because of their knowledge or gifts, particularly their "spiritual gifts." Those gifts had led some of them to believe they understood what it meant to be truly spiritual. It's no accident that, in the middle of Paul's most extended treatment on the church and spiritual giftedness (1 Cor. 12, 14), one finds the most extended treatment of love in the New Testament (1 Cor. 13).

On first reading, chapter 13 can seem like a digression. Why is this beautiful poem on love placed here? But it's not a digression. It's the high point of the whole letter. It's as if Paul is saying, "Don't you see, in all your conflicts and questions (the things you wrote to ask me about), that nothing is more important than love? Don't you see that this is your fundamental problem? You don't *know* what love is!"

The church in Corinth did not see how central, how necessary, love is to those who are in Christ. Without love you have nothing—no matter what else you have. Without love you gain nothing that counts—no matter what else you gain. Without love you are nothing—no matter what you may think you are.

OUR FAILURE TO LOVE

Perhaps we could say with some accuracy, in diagnosing the weaknesses of the church in the West today, that this remains a besetting problem: a failure to love. We still fail even to know what love is, much less how to show it to one another (John 13:35), much less how to show it to the world.

Jesus says that love is the sum of all that is contained in the law of God. All the law and the prophets are summed up in the commands to love God with all your heart, mind, and soul and to love your neighbor as yourself (Matt. 22:37–39). These words can be so familiar that their weight is lost on us. Jesus is telling us that the whole duty of humanity is contained in the command to love.

If our sustained reflection on Scripture, our doctrine, and our theology doesn't lead to lives of love, then it doesn't matter how well we think we *know* what the Scriptures say. If we don't love—in the manner Christ has shown us—then we have missed the point of them all. No matter if we can cite chapter and verse, no matter how accurate our doctrine may be, no matter how credentialed we are, if we don't have love, then the indictment stands: we have nothing.

The whole point of the life God has given us is to become human beings who love. That's the goal: to love God and love others. Which means if we haven't learned how to love on God's terms, then we have missed the point of our one life, no matter what else we've accomplished. If love is the greatest commandment, then that means the greatest failure in life is our failure to love.

Everything God requires of us is comprehended in that one command: love. That's what Paul means when he says, "The whole law is fulfilled in one word: 'You shall love your neighbor as yourself'" (Gal. 5:14).

John writes that if you truly love God the inevitable fruit of that will be loving others. John goes on to single out love as the way we know that we know God. By this we can know that we have come to know God, that we love one another (1 John 4:7–8). Paul says in another place that "the only thing that counts is faith expressing itself through love" (Gal. 5:6 NIV). This complements James, who says that a faith that does not manifest in works of love is a dead faith (James 2:17). Jesus says that love is to be the hallmark by which his followers are known in the world: "By this all people will know that you are my disciples, if you have love for one another" (John 13:35).

One of America's greatest theologians, Jonathan Edwards, wrote a whole book on 1 Corinthians 13 entitled *Charity and Its Fruits*. He writes, "Love appears to be the sum of all the virtue and duty that God requires of us, and therefore must undoubtedly be the most essential thing—the sum of all the virtue that is essential and distinguishing in real Christianity."[8]

Edwards goes on to say that "love is the main principle in the heart of a real Christian" and therefore "the labour of love is the main business of the Christian life."[9] Following Edwards's charge and this litany of Scripture verses, we can ask ourselves, *Is love our main business?*

It's a good sign if you are feeling troubled and uncomfortable right now. If we are beyond being disturbed by such provocations, then we are in sad shape indeed. *Jesus, I didn't really trust what you said so clearly was most important to you.*

Paul wrote 1 Corinthians 13 to unsettle his readers. He was taking the premium that his readers placed on knowledge, and the confidence they had in their own gifts, and then multiplying their accomplishments to the most extreme degree imaginable. You have knowledge? What if you could fathom all mysteries (v. 2)? You have faith? What if your faith could move mountains (v. 2)? Do you believe you are sacrificial and spiritual? What if you gave away all that you had, even your own body to be burned (v. 3)? In the opening verses of chapter 13, Paul names the things his status-hungry readers were most prone to boast in—most prone to lift up and say, "Now I'm something. Look what I have. Look what I've done." Then comes the punch: if you have not love, then you are a zero. "I am nothing" (v. 2). "I gain nothing" (v. 3).

Do you see why we say that 1 Corinthians 13 is one of the most terrifying chapters in the Bible? Paul was saying that you can be incredibly gifted, eloquent, and prophetic; you can be eminently knowledgeable and understand deep mysteries of the faith; you can be zealously committed; you can even be touched by the very spirit of God ... yet not be what Edwards calls "a real Christian." To use terminology the Puritans were fond of, there can be light (knowledge of God) but no heat (truly knowing God, personally and experientially).

Paul turns the Corinthians' zeal for knowledge and accomplishment up to the nth degree and basically says, "It doesn't matter how excellent your performances and gifts are—if you haven't learned how to love, you are nothing." He didn't say, "You missed it" or "You're not quite there." He said, "Nothing."

Paul is taking our desire to make something of our lives and telling us: if we haven't learned what love is and how to do it, then all we have managed to accomplish adds up to nothing.

THE COUP DE GRÂCE

You've heard the phrase *coup de grâce*? It's a French phrase that means "a stroke of grace" or "a blow of mercy." It originally referred to a death blow to end the suffering of a severely wounded person or animal.[10]

That's how we should read 1 Corinthians 13: it's a blow of mercy. It's a stroke of grace that lays us low. If we read this chapter and think, *Love, okay. Got it. Next*, then we have done something far more dangerous to our souls than simply misunderstanding a passage of Scripture. This beautiful hymn to love is meant to wound. It is life-giving trauma. But for it to be life-giving, we have to feel the trauma. It must strike us with great force. This is the most important thing in life, the sum of all my duty to God. When we can acknowledge, "Lord, I have failed to love and must relearn what love really is," that's the cruciform life applied to love.

This is the painful wisdom that von Balthasar was trying to impart to his readers and that my dear old grandfather was trying to impart to me and that de Botton was trying to impart on the pages of the *New York Times*. It's humbling. It lays us low, but being laid low by our failure becomes the path toward becoming people who can build one another up in love. "'Knowledge' puffs up, but love builds up" (1 Cor. 8:1). There's a new life possible on the other side of this most painful acknowledgment: I have failed at what is most important—learning how to love.

If humility is the heart of the cruciform life, then love is the heartbeat, the living sign that the word of the cross has taken root in your heart.

I (Rankin) have a friend who lives in Shanghai next to a hundred-story building. He says that when the skyscraper was being built, they first had to dig five floors into the ground. That's a parable: the higher a building would rise, the deeper the hole must go for the foundation.

We too must go down before we can rise up. "Deeper, deeper in the love of Jesus / Daily let me go," an old gospel song puts it.[11] We are going *down* into this painful self-knowledge. But that's also the way up. The path goes down, down, deeper into the love of Jesus, as we let God love us as we are, and then—what's even harder—we must learn how to remain (abide) in that posture of dependence. Only then can we love one another, as Jesus first loved us (John 15:12). How can I love my enemy until I've sensed that I too was God's enemy, yet he first loved me?

LOVE IS WHAT LOVE DOES

Lewis Smedes is another author who has written an entire book on just the thirteenth chapter of 1 Corinthians.[12] John Piper says that Smedes's book, *Love within Limits*, "gives more insight into the *reality* talked about in 1 Corinthians 13 than ten technical commentaries combined."[13]

By Smedes's count, Paul highlights fourteen facets of love in this short chapter like fourteen different faces of one diamond. In order to catch a glimpse of what cruciform love looks like, let's look briefly at only the first two facets: "love is patient" and "love is kind" (v. 4 NASB).

Commentators point out that English can't quite catch the nuances, but in the original language these descriptors are verbs, not adjectives, as we are prone to think of them. It's not that love *is* patient—it's that love practices patience. It's not that love is kind, but that love manifests kindness.

Love is what love does.

Cruciform Love Is Patient

Patience is the ability to endure suffering, frustration, and disappointment gracefully, without reacting or lashing out. Patience does more than listen attentively; patience bears with the shortcomings of others in a spirit of gentleness and humility. Humility because to become patient requires a keen sense of your own shortcomings and your own tendency to disappoint others. And gentleness because to become patient means to stay engaged, focused on the hurts and concerns of the other without becoming defensive or resentful. This explains why *patience* is sometimes translated "long-suffering" and is sometimes coupled with *gentleness* and *humility*. "I … urge you to walk … with all humility and gentleness, with patience, bearing with one another in love" (Eph. 4:1–2).

Patience in our relationships has to do with how we respond to unmet expectations, even when those expectations were reasonable and fair. You are a parent and your child deliberately defies your clearly expressed will. You are a supervisor and an employee keeps making the same mistake. You are a coach and a player keeps blowing the same assignment.

In those situations a patient person doesn't react. He or she feels disappointed, yes, but chooses in that moment to bear the disappointment internally rather than lashing out and expressing it externally, all the while remembering that a great deal of our communication is nonverbal. It's possible to guard our mouths (Ps. 141:3) but still communicate impatience very clearly to those around us.

One way to know that you are growing in patience is that when others disappoint you, it doesn't rob you of your peace. You don't obsess over the thoughtlessness or carelessness of others. Patience can present as outer calm because you've done a great deal of hard inner work. You know you are growing in patience the more you are willing to let go of an argument or delay having your say.

That's very different from our normal relational patterns, which go something like this: "I'll love you as long as you meet my expectations and don't disappoint me." But true love is patient. It stays present in the face of frustrated expectations. You're not defensive because you choose to be focused on the other. You care more about understanding the other than being understood yourself. Being understood can wait until *after* the other feels heard and cared for—even when that person was the one who let *you* down! Think how many arguments could be defused if you choose a patient spirit (Prov. 16:32).

If the first mark of love is a patient, long-suffering spirit, how are you doing? How willing are you to bear the faults of others with gentleness and humility and without reacting in irritation or anger? Most of us can stop right here at the top of the list and say, "God, I don't see that in my heart."

Okay. Do you want it to be? Would you like to go through life with patience? Doesn't that sound as if it is connected to happiness? Doesn't that sound good and beautiful?

Cruciform Love Is Kind

Patience and kindness are listed as two sides of the same coin. Patience concerns how we respond to people, and kindness concerns how we approach or move toward people.

Empathy is a word in vogue today. Empathy is also hard work. It is the hard, imaginative work of stepping into the shoes of others, working to understand why they feel the way they do, why they think that way, or why they responded that way. Empathy is rare. But kindness is even rarer, as it goes beyond empathy.

Kindness sees with discerning clarity but uses that discernment to move toward others in compassion. Kindness moves toward people in whom you are disappointed or whom you know are disappointed in you.

In his book *The Emotional Life of Our Lord*, B. B. Warfield noted that compassion is the emotion most frequently attributed to Jesus in the gospels.[14] Jesus prayed from the cross, "Father, forgive them, for they know not what they do" (Luke 23:34). That's the Bible's signature line of kindness. Kindness is empathy plus compassion. It moves *toward* others in empathy and compassion, not *away* in judgment.

A kind heart says, "I see your faults, but I choose to believe that this is not who you want to be." A kind heart is disposed to give the other the benefit of the doubt, even to assume the best, which is the opposite of our default posture, what Paul calls the "old self" (Eph. 4:22). The old self gives ourselves the benefit of the doubt ("I'm tired and hungry" or "They don't understand") but is exacting with others. The old self is fond of justice meted out to others and often speaks in judicial language of what's right or what others deserve.

Stephen Covey tells a story in *The 7 Habits of Highly Effective People* of a man on the subway whose kids are acting wildly, screaming and crawling all over the car, while the man just sits with his eyes closed. The other passengers are angry that the father is letting his children run loose … until it is revealed that they're coming from the hospital where the children's mother has just died.[15]

You could ask, "How could the other passengers have known the burdens this man was carrying?" But that's the point: a kind person is predisposed to think, *Be kind. For everyone you meet is fighting a hard battle.*[16]

Some in our culture have the perception that kindness means weakness, as though being kind is the opposite of being strong. In reality, it takes tremendous strength and uncommon courage to be kind, to move toward the other, especially when the other offers nothing in return or views you with suspicion, mistrust, and even ill will.

"Kindness is risky," Smedes says.[17] It risks opening yourself up to being misunderstood or even taken advantage of. It's kindness that turns the other cheek (Matt. 5:39). Kindness is not a blank check that countenances abuse—nothing would be unkinder than to allow another to persist in such self-destructive behavior. But love that is kind refuses to give up on unlovely, unkind, and even mean-spirited people. Kindness bears the injustice as Christ did on the cross. You bear the injustice. That's why love, true love, cruciform love, must always be kind *and* patient.

Kindness is not being nice.[18] Kindness risks not being liked in order to be a voice of healing. The test of kindness is that you see but you stay. You stay engaged with the other, deeply aware of the "log that is in your own eye" (Matt. 7:3), because you are promised that then you'll be able to see clearly and help others from that place of empathy plus compassion (v. 5). There's nothing soft about kindness. Only the brave can be kind. Kindness requires deep self-awareness of our own tendency to be self-righteous. Our compassion for the other, our care, emerges from a deep sense of our own frailty.

Accordingly, the best evidence of a kind heart is the actual demonstration of kindness. Love manifests kindness. Love is kindness, not only to your friends (Jesus says anyone can do that) but also to your enemies. Love that is cruciform keeps moving toward the unlovely, the disagreeable, and the unkind. You move toward people who are not your friends and are not being friendly toward you. That's cruciform love.[19]

LORD, MAKE ME AN INSTRUMENT OF THY LOVE

We are only two descriptors into Paul's list of attributes of love in 1 Corinthians 13! Do we dare to keep reading? The first two have already laid us low, and we haven't even gotten to "is not irritable or resentful," "is not arrogant or rude," and "does not insist on its own way." Already do we not need to cry out, "Lord Jesus Christ, have mercy on me, a sinner!"?

Our gospel is that before Jesus asked us to bear the injustice that kindness and patience call for, our Lord bore that injustice himself. On the cross Jesus did not call down the fire of judgment that we deserved. Rather, he endured it in our place. Before he called us to be patient, he was long-suffering, even to the point of death. Before he asked us to be kind, Jesus was and is kind toward us. Jesus became the one who suffers *with*. He saw our unloveliness, yet he did not withdraw. He came near, and on the cross, he stayed.

Abiding in Christ is the catalyst that can transform our impatient, unkind hearts. If God can continue to be so patient with me, given my debt to him, how could I not be patient with others, no matter their debts to me? Or would we rather God treat us the way we treat others in those many instances when we find ourselves being impatient, unkind, and unforgiving?

When we are confronted with the miracle that God could love us—that this is what love is—we are laid low. When we personally experience the patience and kindness of God toward us, we are forced to ask, "Have I ever loved anyone in my life?" God's amazing love for us calls us, again and again and again, to relearn what love—cruciform love—really is.

Alain de Botton was right that so many of our relational frustrations come from the fact that we don't understand what love is. But he was wrong in saying that no "perfect being exists who can meet all our needs."[20] His prescription is one of pessimism and resignation: stop hoping that anyone could ever love you like that! But the gospel tells us there *is* a perfect being who meets all our deepest needs (Phil. 4:19).

UNION WITH CHRIST MAKES LOVE POSSIBLE

Not only does Jesus pronounce his love over us; he also unites our lives to his. I (Rankin) used to read 1 Corinthians 13 and get incredibly depressed. I'd be forced to conclude, *I'm not like that. I'll never be like that. It's not in me to love like that.* And there's a deep truth there. We don't have it in us naturally to be patient and kind.

But when you know Christ, you have the ability to be patient and kind. Jesus has been patient and kind with us to a degree that is beyond imagining. When his perfect patience and kindness for you take root, that is the beginning of a new life—his life—in you. So now in Christ you do have it in you to be patient and kind, because you have Christ in you (Col. 1:27). Christ in you enables you to love others as he has loved you.

And not only *can* he do this, but he also intends to do this. He is willing and he is able. "Love enables us to do what love obligates us to do."[21] Without the gospel 1 Corinthians 13 will humble you into the dust. With the gospel it becomes the most beautiful portrait of possibility in the Bible. Here is the type of person Jesus died to make you into and intends to transform you into if you will more and more surrender to his love, deeper and deeper into the love of Jesus, daily let me go.

That makes every failure of your love in your relationships an opportunity to rehearse the goodness of the gospel toward you. The next time you find yourself disappointed (which happens every day!), instead of blowing up or lashing out, you can exercise patience, that ability to endure, to bear with. Instead of withdrawing, kindness stays and moves toward. The people you're dealing with know not what they do.

How do you bring heat to this light? Every relational conflict is an invitation to receive God's love for you. God was infinitely patient with you, and this ought to make you so gentle with others. What others do to me once and in small measure, I do to God all the time. Yet he sees and stays. Jesus is patient. Jesus is kind. And those who abide in his life can become those who learn how to love in God's way, the cruciform way.

CRUCIFORM SUFFERING

Of all the chapters in this book, this one is the most difficult to write. It's difficult, because it can be so easy to write falsely about suffering. And it's dangerous to write falsely about suffering, because it can lead us to misunderstand who God is for us.

Suffering strikes at the heart of our sense of meaning and purpose. For those faced with grief, depression, abuse, oppression, injustice, illness, or chronic pain, suffering can raise some of the most difficult existential questions—not only whether life is *good*, but whether life is even worth living.

Thus we come to this chapter in fear and trembling.

We have been arguing that the way of the cross is the way to true human flourishing. This is a shocking claim because the cross is an instrument of suffering and death. It's hard to imagine how the cross could have any place in the good life. Most of the time we think life is good when we are not suffering, and we do whatever we can to avoid suffering.

Yet suffering is unavoidable. It is common to all humanity: pain, illness, and loss, as well as personal crises in family, friendships, and work. There are other forms of suffering that are all too common but afflict some people more than others: violence, abuse, injustice, and oppression. There are also uniquely Christian forms of suffering, that of suffering for the sake of Christ: this is the suffering of dying to oneself, of dying to the world, of persecution and martyrdom.

This chapter explores what the cross shows us about all three of these forms of suffering. First, the cross shows us God's solidarity with us in suffering. Second, the cross shows us that God is for those who suffer injustice, and that the cross is the means by which God sets things right in the world. Third, we will see that the way of the cross is one of suffering specifically for Christ—but that we are not alone in this suffering.

JESUS AMONG THE PHILOSOPHERS: SUFFERING AND THE GOOD LIFE

Seneca writes, "Life is filled and plagued with a variety of misfortunes, which grant no one a lasting peace, scarcely even a truce."[1]

Suffering is part of the human condition. There is no avoiding it. We are fragile creatures, vulnerable to illness and accident, disease and death, heartbreak and grief. None of us would include these things in our vision of the good life. And yet there is simply no way to escape suffering entirely.

The ancients were no strangers to suffering. They were arguably more intimately acquainted with it than we are now. They lived with no modern medicine, no vaccinations or painkillers. Childbirth always presented the possibility of death—for mother as well as child—and children often died before adulthood. Famine, plague, and enslavement by conquering enemies were ever-present possibilities.

As a consequence, Greek and Roman philosophers had to tackle the question, "What does the art of living have to say about suffering?" This question was urgent—and like suffering, unavoidable. Any philosopher claiming to offer the true art of living had to confront the reality of suffering.

Some were quite blunt. Aristotle, one of the greatest thinkers of human happiness (*eudaimonia*), argues that some people cannot be happy because certain kinds of misfortune will cripple your happiness: if you're born to a bad family, if you're ugly or deformed, or live alone or childless, you can't really be called happy.[2] Financial ruin, the death of your friends, or foolish children can also undermine your happiness. Too much suffering, and your life simply isn't going to be a happy one. The best people will bear these burdens nobly and maintain a certain degree of happiness, but their life is not going to be what Aristotle calls blessed[3] (*makarios*—the same word Jesus uses in the Sermon on the Mount). That's just how life goes for some people.

Other philosophers argue that these external circumstances don't matter. You can be happy in any circumstance, because virtue alone is sufficient for happiness. The Cynics thought that most people value the wrong things—money, comfort, status—and as a result they suffer. Similarly, the Stoics believed suffering is the false belief that one's circumstances are bad, when, in fact, everything happens the way it should. There is a providential order—whether we call it the will of the gods, Zeus, or nature—that ensures everything happens as it's supposed to. This is true for illness, personal ruin—even the death of a child.[4] The goal of Stoic life was to accept everything that is not up to us, and focus instead on what is up to us—our judgments, passions, and choices—in order to achieve an ideal state of tranquility (*apatheia*).

The Epicureans also sought an ideal of mental tranquility and freedom from disturbance—what they called *ataraxia*. They saw this as the highest state of pleasure, and all it requires is a simple, contemplative life. According to Epicurus, this is how the gods live. They are not concerned with human affairs, because they live in their own distant realm, enjoying their own state of perfect bliss. As such, they give us an example for our own happiness, tranquility, and freedom from disturbance.

The recurring theme among these philosophers is that the answer to suffering is to change our way of thinking. Suffering is to be overcome by viewing it in the right way. Some of their achievements are truly remarkable. Take Epicurus: on the last day of his life, he wrote a letter to his friend Idomeneus describing what he calls "a blessedly happy day." He had suffered for two agonizing weeks from a kidney stone that blocked his urinary tract. He describes a constant suffering with no relief, but against all these sufferings he sets "a gladness of mind at the remembrance of our past conversations."[5]

It's hard not to be impressed by this composure. It's a remarkable feat and a testimony to what the human mind can achieve with discipline. But there's also a kind of despair in it. These philosophers were trying to protect themselves against suffering by detaching themselves, and denying the reality of suffering—that it really is what it seems to be: bad. Thinking differently was the best option they could offer. It wasn't safe for them to recognize suffering for what it is, because they had no reason to hope for anything better.

When Christianity entered the ancient world, it told a very different story. Unlike the gods of Epicurus, the God of the Bible is not distant from human concerns, living in his own indifferent bliss. Jesus is God's response to suffering. God became human, and being fully human he suffered. God submitted to the same constraints of all suffering flesh: hunger, thirst, fatigue, temptation, and death.

In Jesus, God looks suffering square in the face. Jesus is braver and more honest than any of the philosophers. He enters a world of chronic pain, debilitating disease, of children and friends who die. He sees it all, and says that this is not how things are supposed to be. When Jesus arrives at the tomb of his friend Lazarus, he weeps. He is deeply moved and greatly troubled (John 11:33, 35).

Jesus wept. This verse is so brief, it is easy to overlook just how different Jesus is compared with the sages of Greco-Roman philosophy. The sages of Stoic and Epicurean philosophy argue that death is not to be feared because it is a natural part of life. Epicurus argues that "death is nothing to us"; it's simply the end of consciousness.[6] While Socrates was awaiting his execution, he argued that death is a good thing because it sets the soul free from the prison of the body. Socrates admonished his friends for weeping.[7] But Jesus wept with and for his friends.

Facing death, Socrates and Jesus are worlds apart. In his final hours, Socrates was surrounded by his friends, engaged in dialogue about why death is nothing to fear. In his final hours, Jesus was alone in prayer. His disciples had fallen asleep. One had already betrayed him. When he was arrested, the rest abandoned him. Another denied him three times. Jesus was in anguish. Whereas Socrates embraced his cup of hemlock, Jesus prayed, "If it be possible, let this cup pass from me" (Matt. 26:39). And on the cross, Jesus did not exhibit Stoic apatheia, but instead the full passion of suffering and death. He cried out in his experience of separation from the Father: "My God, my God, why have you forsaken me?" (Matt. 27:46). This is a full, honest confrontation with suffering and death.

Jesus does not merely give us a different way to think about our suffering. Jesus allows us to recognize suffering for what it is, and to see that it grieves the heart of God.

Hebrews 2:9 tells us that Jesus tasted death for all. Those who suffer can know that God is not a distant, dispassionate observer but a God who endured suffering and death himself. The cross is God's solidarity with human suffering.

Better still, after a Saturday of silence,[8] the resurrection proved that the cross was God's victory over death. Not only did Jesus undergo death; he defeated death by death. Those who are in Christ participate in his death, but they also participate in his resurrection. Those who die with him also rise with him.

The next verse in Hebrews makes an equally astounding claim: "It was fitting that he, for whom and by whom all things exist, in bringing many sons to glory, should make the founder of their salvation perfect through suffering" (Heb. 2:10). Jesus was made perfect, brought to completion through his suffering.

There have been heresies that held that Jesus' suffering was not really suffering—that it was all appearance and that he was removed from the suffering. Otherwise he wouldn't really be God, the thinking goes. But Hebrews is arguing that the suffering was not only real but also fitting, even necessary, for bringing even Christ to completion. "Although he was a son, he learned obedience through what he suffered" (Heb. 5:8). That it was proper, fitting, and necessary for Christ to suffer tells us something essential about the Lord we worship. His suffering was not incidental or accidental. And as we will see below, this is crucial for understanding the meaning of our own suffering.

When we are in the darkest nights of suffering, when we feel forsaken by God, we can know that we are not alone. Jesus has experienced that Godforsakenness on the cross. At the cross, Jesus suffered the separation of Father from Son. Because of the cross, God knows the loss of a son. And the Son knows the suffering of separation from a father as well as the experience of the absence of

God and the silence of God. Jesus has experienced this firsthand and is with us in this experience.

Through this suffering, however, Jesus was perfected—made complete (Heb. 2:10; 5:9).

If Jesus was perfected through his suffering, then we can see how God also uses suffering to bring us to completion. James writes that you should "count it all joy … when you meet trials of various kinds, for you know that the testing of your faith produces steadfastness. And let steadfastness have its full effect, that you may be perfect and complete, lacking in nothing" (1:2–4). Similarly, Peter writes, "Since therefore Christ suffered in the flesh, arm yourselves with the same way of thinking, for whoever has suffered in the flesh has ceased from sin" (1 Pet. 4:1). Paul writes that we should even rejoice in our suffering because "suffering produces endurance, and endurance produces character, and character produces hope" (Rom. 5:3–4).

For the New Testament writers, God uses suffering to bring us to completion in Christ. This point is the key for interpreting the oft-cited verse, Romans 8:28: "We know that God causes all things to work together for good to those who love God, to those who are called according to His purpose" (NASB). This verse is often interpreted as a promise that God is always going to bring the believer out on top and that things are always going to "work out for the best." This can easily go in the direction of the theology of glory, even the prosperity gospel. When God closes a door, the saying goes, he opens a window. If I lose a job, I should take heart that God will work out another job for me.

But what is the *good* in question in verse 28? Contrary to the prosperity-gospel interpretation, we need to keep reading through verse 29: "For those whom He foreknew, He also pre-destined to become conformed to the image of His Son, so that He would be the firstborn among many brethren" (NASB). The good in question is that the Christian will be conformed to the image of Christ. That is what we are made for and that is where we will find our deepest joy.

Throughout the Bible, we find the recurring theme that God turns mourning into joy, even dancing (Ps. 30:11; Jer. 31:13), and sorrow into joy (John 16:22). The prophet promises that God will wipe away every tear (Isa. 25:8; Rev. 7:17). But the psalmist adds that there is a joy only made possible by having gone through the pain. This is the hope of the psalmist that "those who sow in tears shall reap with shouts of joy" (Ps. 126:5).

EVIL: PROBLEM OR MYSTERY?

These are God's promises to those who suffer. There is hope. But hope cannot be turned into a system, a logic that answers all our questions and resolves what philosophers call the problem of evil, or what C. S. Lewis called the problem of pain.

Epicurus is credited with being the first to spell out the logical problem that evil and suffering seem to pose: roughly, if God is perfectly good and all-powerful, then why is there evil? It seems like a good God should get rid of evil, so maybe he can't. But if he can—and doesn't—then maybe he isn't fully good.

Philosophers have spent a lot of time on this problem, and have come up with some satisfactory responses. But a satisfactory response to the logical problem of evil still leaves the existential experience of evil and suffering untouched. In the crucible, answers aren't very satisfying.[9] This is why the philosopher Gabriel Marcel argues that it's a mistake to frame evil as a *problem* and that it is better understood as *mystery*. A problem is a puzzle to be solved, a question to be answered with the right information. Mystery is something else. Marcel doesn't mean mystery in the sense of a mystery novel, where the right clue will suddenly unravel the mystery. Mystery in Marcel's sense is not a lack of information, but a surplus of reality. When I reduce suffering to a problem to be solved logically, I quickly find I'm no longer talking about what people are actually experiencing. In Marcel's words, "The problem disintegrates, loses all meaning, the moment it is transformed into an academic question."[10]

The experience of suffering so often prompts the question *Why?* Why me? Why this? Why now? Why do bad things happen to good people? It's easy to mistake this why question as a request for an abstract answer, some bit of information that will resolve the questioning. The challenge for the philosopher, pastor, family member, or friend, is to find a way to respond to this question concretely and sympathetically. Thus Marcel writes that the "problem" of evil and suffering "cannot be dealt with except in the context of a concrete communication of one person with another."[11] This means being *with* the other person, inhabiting the place of suffering with them. This is the meaning of compassion—literally, "suffering with"—the other person.

This is the way that God addresses those who suffer. Scripture never offers a theoretical answer, an abstract "solution" to the problem of evil. Instead of giving us an abstract answer, God gives us himself. In Christ, God enters into our suffering and takes it upon himself and into his own life. If we want to see God's response to the mystery of evil and suffering, we need to look at Jesus. The living Christ is our hope.

Some people will see this hope fulfilled, their mourning turned to joy, in this life. Sometimes, like Joseph in Genesis, we're allowed to see God's redemptive use of the evil intended against us (Gen. 50:20). And Jesus went about healing sicknesses and disease to show us that God is making all things new. The redemptive pattern has already begun. But still, it must be admitted, there are some evils so horrendous or enduring that their sorrow and anguish will only be extinguished in the next life, in the infinite goodness of full communion with God.[12] The cross shows us the possibility of healing and redemption in this life and the certainty of healing and redemption in the next life.

SUFFERING INJUSTICE

The missionary Chrissie Chapman has spent many years serving in the African country of Burundi. She tells the story of an eighty-four-year-old man she saw sitting in the dirt as she was distributing porridge to displaced people in a camp. He had walked down from the mountains, twenty kilometers over five days, and he told how his entire family had been killed in the civil war—his wife, their five children, as well as their families. His house had also been destroyed, and he escaped with nothing more than the clothes he was wearing. As she gave him food, he told her, "Madam missionary, I never realized that Jesus was all I needed, until Jesus was all I had."[13]

Stories like this are inspiring. But they raise another, difficult question. For those who have lost everything, the crucified Jesus is their only consolation. But is the crucified Jesus *only* consolation? What does the cross have to say to those who are suffering from injustice, under oppression, living in repressive regimes, afflicted by violence, or enduring poverty? Is cruciform faith merely an opiate, as Marx would have it—a painkiller that eases the symptoms, but leaves the causes in place? Some critics argue that the cross actually *hinders* justice, since it encourages people to suffer patiently rather than actively resisting injustice.

This question needs serious consideration, because there are many cases in which the cross has not represented justice, but rather its opposite. This is an objection that has historically hung over the discussion of the theology of the cross.[14]

The cross is, after all, a dangerous symbol. Early in this book, we saw how the Romans intended the cross as an instrument of violent oppression. It was a means of invoking fear and exercising total power over their subjects. Jesus' death on the cross took this symbol of violence and power and transformed its meaning. Nevertheless, we need to confront the fact that the cross remains an ambiguous symbol. Even after Christ's resurrection, the cross has continued to be used by some as a symbol of violence and oppression or to enforce existing human power, not only in the Roman world but also as the sword of Constantine, the emblem of the Crusades, a symbol of anti-Semitism, and the burning crosses of the KKK. We want to state clearly: this is not the cross of Christ.

The cross is also dangerous when misused by Christian preaching and teaching to praise weakness and suffering in a distorted way or to sanction the status quo.

Critics in feminist and liberation theology have leveled this charge against the theology of the cross: perhaps those who are in positions of power and privilege need to learn the way of weakness, suffering, and humility. But for those suffering abuse, violence, and injustice, this kind of talk is a luxury they cannot afford. Instead of bringing justice and peace, the cross teaches victims to be patient rather than to resist injustice, critics say. It teaches them to see violence and abuse as their "cross to bear." It allows injustice to go unchecked and so is anything but good news to the poor and most vulnerable among us.

We take this objection seriously. It deserves a book of its own, not a portion of a chapter. For now, though, we want to make a few brief points in respectful dialogue.

First, it is the consistent witness of Scripture that God hears the cries of those who suffer injustice. God heard his people when they were slaves in Egypt (Ex. 2:23–25). He heard them in exile, scattered in Babylon and Assyria. He heard them when they were under Roman rule. God has mercy on those who are poor and oppressed, on prisoners and those who are denied justice. If you read the Hebrew prophets, there is no mistaking the fact that God's heart is for justice. He is not interested in our religious worship when it overlooks the poor and is allied with oppression (Isa. 1:11–17).

This is the God who became human and read Isaiah 61:1 aloud in the synagogue: "The Spirit of the Lord is upon me, because he has anointed me to proclaim good news to the poor. He has sent me to proclaim liberty to the captives and recovering of sight to the blind, to set at liberty those who are oppressed, to proclaim the year of the Lord's favor" (Luke 4:18–19).

Jesus identifies himself as the fulfilment of this prophecy. He is both the prophet and the fulfillment of Israel's hope for a messiah who would deliver them. But he did not fulfill this hope like they expected. Jesus' hearers expected that the messiah, like a true son of David, would be a mighty military leader to overthrow Roman power. Instead, the way of Jesus as the messiah leads to the cross.

The cross shows just how seriously God takes injustice. God became human and suffered with us, not only in his death but also in his life. He suffered not only the cross, but also in his birth in a stable, childhood as a refugee, life of poverty in a backwater town under a repressive regime. He was betrayed and then abandoned, falsely accused and then endured an unjust trial. His whole life, from beginning to end, showed solidarity with those who suffer unjustly.

But the cross is not only an act of solidarity. It is also the means by which God set things right in the world, establishing justice and peace between himself and the world. This is how God reconciled the sinful world to himself (Col. 1:20). It is also how he reconciles sinners to other sinners: through forgiveness, not violence.

Second, at the cross Jesus set things right in the world, but he did this in the most unusual way. The cross is not only the means of our deliverance—it frames the method for our mission to the world.[15] He did not fight fire with fire or power with power. This is where the theology of the cross is vulnerable to the critique that this emphasis on weakness does not *empower* those who are really weak. Thus, it would seem dangerous for us to write about the crucifixion of the ego, as we have above. This kind of language may seem disempowering. How does this empower the poor and the vulnerable? It could easily be (and has been) used to sanction the status quo and suppress those not in power. "Humble your pride" can be distorted into "Don't speak up for yourself or speak out for the sake of others."

But we need to be very careful here. If the theology of the cross is dangerous, so is the language of empowerment. Nietzsche shows us how easily a righteous cause can be a mask for revenge and an indirect way of gaining power.[16] What exactly is the power we are after? Where does it come from? What gives the power for self-assertion? These questions go to the heart of many of the social, cultural, and political revolutions of world history. If the goal of empowerment is simply to affirm our egos as they are, without confronting the sin in ourselves, then whatever power is gained is just going to continue in the same cycle of oppression. The tables may be turned, but nothing really changes. The victim becomes the new victimizer.

That sort of empowerment is still the old Roman logic: the way to victory is to gain power over your enemy. That is how the principalities and powers of the world work. But at the cross Jesus overcame principalities and powers—not by overpowering them but by suffering under them and showing the true nature of things: the way of peace, love, and forgiveness. The cross calls sin what it is: rebellion against both God and the world as God has created it to be. This sober realism in turn gives us the clarity and the courage to call sin what it is—in the world and in ourselves.

SUFFERING AND DISCIPLESHIP

Of all the startling things that happen in the book of Acts, one of the most remarkable is the conversion of Saul, better known as Paul. Saul was hostile to the early church, persecuting the disciples with such zeal that Scripture describes him as "breathing ... murder" against them (Acts 9:1). After Saul's conversion on the road to Damascus, God told Ananias, one of the believers from that city, to go help Saul. Ananias was understandably worried because Saul's reputation had preceded him, but God assured Ananias: "Go, for he is a chosen instrument of mine.... I will show him how much he must suffer for the sake of my name" (vv. 15–16).

What a thing to hear! Imagine what the newly converted Saul's response would have been if he had heard this word. He seems to have gotten the message, though, because suffering became a central motif throughout his letters. The New Testament is filled with the theme of suffering, and almost every letter of Paul's contains his reflections and exhortations regarding suffering.

Paul wrote so much about suffering because it was a regular feature of his life and in the lives of the early Christians. It remains true that for those who follow in the way of Jesus, suffering will come. Paul wrote to encourage his fellow believers, because no one envisions suffering as part of the good life. We would prefer to be spared suffering.

This was true in the New Testament, and it is true now. We see this in a pivotal conversation between Jesus and Peter: "From that time Jesus began to show his disciples that he must go to Jerusalem and suffer many things from the elders and chief priests and scribes, and be killed, and on the third day be raised. And Peter took him aside and began to rebuke him, saying, 'Far be it from you, Lord! This shall never happen to you.' But he turned and said to Peter, 'Get behind me, Satan! You are a hindrance to me. For you are not setting your mind on the things of God, but on the things of man'" (Matt. 16:21–23).

This is Peter grappling with the scandal of the cross. He gives what seems like the most natural, most human, most humane response of a sympathetic friend: "God forbid it, Lord!" Or as Kierkegaard paraphrases it, "Spare yourself."[17] That's why Jesus' reply is so startling: "Get behind Me, Satan! You are a stumbling block"—an offense, a *skandalon*—"to Me" (v. 23 NASB).

Kierkegaard's point is that what seemed like the greatest love of one friend for another was in fact a temptation. Peter wanted Jesus to spare himself the cross. That sounds like a mercy, but in view of the kingdom of God, it would've been disastrous. Without the cross, Christianity would not exist. Without the cross, there would be no gospel, no deliverance, no reconciliation, no freedom. All that is good about the good news would be impossible without the cross.

This is a temptation for every Christian: to conceive of Christianity without the cross. Suffering is part of the Christian's journey. This is why Jesus immediately turned to his disciples and said, "If anyone would come after me, let him deny himself and take up his cross and follow me. For whoever would save his life will lose it, but whoever loses his life for my sake will find it" (vv. 24–25).

There is no Christianity without the cross. Thus, there is no Christianity without suffering.

Suffering, as we've said, is part of every human life, but the New Testament is also concerned with a uniquely Christian suffering, which is the suffering that inevitably comes from taking up one's cross and following Christ. Cruciform suffering encompasses both the suffering that happens to us but also the suffering we undergo *for the sake of* Christ.

This is not a pleasant thought. Many of us would probably prefer to ignore this idea or pretend it isn't central to Christianity. Yet Jesus told his disciples that they would be hated by all for his name's sake (Matt. 10:22; Mark 13:13; Luke 21:17). Jesus tells us this, yet it is easy for us to forget it. Or maybe to ignore it. Or deny it. As Dietrich Bonhoeffer observes, "From its very beginning the church has taken offense at the suffering Christ. It does not want that kind of Lord."[18] We don't want that kind of Lord because we don't want that kind of life.

Bonhoeffer makes this point in his book *The Cost of Discipleship*. Christians are called to follow after Christ, who is the example, the paradigm or prototype of true humanity. "To this you have been called, because Christ also suffered for you, leaving you an example, so that you might follow in his steps" (1 Pet. 2:21).[19]

According to Bonhoeffer, distinctly Christian suffering—what he calls "Christ-suffering"—begins with the call of Jesus to follow him. Following him cannot be separated from taking up the cross. Thus, the cross is not the culmination of an otherwise happy religious life; it is the point of departure, "the beginning of community with Jesus Christ."[20]

Dying to Self

The first form of uniquely Christian suffering is dying to ourselves for Christ's sake. This is distinct from the general human principle of self-denial that applies to everyone. I need to deny my impulses and appetites if I'm going to be fit, stay healthy, and maintain relationships and a job. But this kind of self-denial can still be rooted in a fundamentally self-serving attitude.

In *Works of Love* Kierkegaard writes that the worldly, "merely human" idea of self-denial is that if you "give up your self-loving desires, cravings, and plans—then you will be esteemed and honored and loved as righteous and wise."[21] According to Kierkegaard, the world's understanding of self-denial is "sagacious"[22]—that is, it is calculating and expects to be understood and honored.

When Jesus calls us to deny ourselves, he is not talking about merely denying ourselves this or that pleasure, giving up a life of partying, or being more considerate of others. Those may be good things, but Jesus is not calling on us to simply change our behaviors. Dying to self goes much deeper, down to the level of our basic posture in life: it means giving up our basic orientation of incurvature, the flesh. It means giving up the lie that I am my own. It means giving up the illusion that the path to happiness is one of serving myself.

Thus, as Kierkegaard writes, "*The Christian idea of self-denial* is: give up your self-loving desires and cravings, give up your self-seeking plans and purposes so that you truly work unselfishly for the good—and then, for that very reason, put up with being abominated almost as a criminal, insulted and ridiculed."[23] The first part is often difficult: "work unselfishly for the good." But the world will often praise you for that. To work for the good and *then* be misunderstood and rejected by the world—that is a scandal to human understanding.

Dying to the World

This brings us to the second form of uniquely Christian suffering: dying to the world.

Dying to the world means dying to our worldly attachments (1 John 2:15–17). This too is suffering. One of the most difficult of these attachments is our desire for the approval of the world. Bonhoeffer emphasizes that Christian suffering is inseparable from rejection. One way we try to save our lives is by trying to save our reputation, status, and prestige. We want to be liked. Yet Jesus tells us that we will be hated (John 15:18–19). Thus, "a disciple is a disciple only in suffering and being rejected, thereby participating in crucifixion."[24]

For many North American Christians, this idea of suffering is a stumbling block. In the past it was more common to interpret the idea of dying to self and the world in terms of giving up certain vices or making lifestyle changes. So being a Christian was seen as square or uncool. But now those look like the good old days. Increasingly, being a Christian is seen as being a villain, as allying oneself with injustice and bigotry, as identifying oneself with the source of colonialism and the Crusades.[25] And for some Christians, sadly, these labels are not undeserved. But we are witnessing a cultural shift. Today Christianity often appears to be not merely uncool or naive but dangerous, even evil.

This shift is not without precedent. In antiquity the Roman historian Tacitus writes that Christians were persecuted not merely for the rumors that circulated about them being responsible for the burning of Rome but more fundamentally for *odium totius generis humani*—"hatred of mankind."[26] Nero made scapegoats of the Christians and condemned them to gruesome, highly theatrical deaths: "Covered with hides of wild beasts, they perished by being torn to pieces by dogs; or they would be fastened to crosses and, when daylight had gone, burned to provide lighting at night."[27]

This is a grim prospect and quite distant from the lives of most North American Christians. We have enjoyed a fairly safe and secure place in the surrounding culture. Thus, Christians should not be too quick to call every obstacle "persecution," because in light of what some brothers and sisters are experiencing around the world, that sounds a lot like entitled complaining. At the same time, many Christians are starting to find that following Jesus has a more immediate and tangible cost: the loss of relationships, career opportunities, social status, and more.

This is a different sort of challenge, and it is important to recognize it for its own distinctive features. It's obnoxious to cry "Persecution!" at every turn, but it's naive to suggest that because North American Christians are not facing prison, torture, or death, there is nothing to see here.

The world has different ways of opposing Christ, and one of the cleverest is for the world to call itself Christian. This is what Kierkegaard calls "Christendom." In Kierkegaard's Denmark this was a result of having an established state church. Being a Danish citizen almost inevitably meant being a Christian. Being a Christian became a matter of being a good, upstanding citizen. You were baptized, married, and buried in the church. Perhaps you went to church at Christmas and Easter. Therefore you were a Christian.

A similar confusion has historically been common in America, where God has been identified with traditional American values. Being a Christian has been considered to be a part of being a good American. One identifies as a Christian for surveys and polls, and the word *evangelical* has come to represent a sociopolitical affiliation rather than a living, active faith.

The problem with Christendom thus defined is that it teaches that you can be a Christian and still be fully at home in the world. When the world and Christianity are on such good terms, it can be difficult to see where they diverge. Being a good Christian looks a lot like being a good American. And thus, being a good American can be taken to mean you are being a good Christian. It can be difficult to see where one ends and the other begins, and as a result it becomes easy to adopt the values of one's culture without recognizing when they are in fact antithetical to the way of Jesus. We get seduced into thinking the American way is the Jesus way and that the American dream is Jesus' plan for us all.

The definition of "good" looks different depending on one's peer group, depending on where you are on the political spectrum. But no one is immune to the blurring of lines between what one's peer group or tribe defines as good and right and what is ultimately good and right according to God.[28] We start to think it should be possible to be a Christian and still have the approval of our culture—that there should be no social cost.

Instead of the both/and of Christendom, the cross presents a clear either/or. We have come to expect that we can have it both ways. In some ways this is more dangerous to faith than outright persecution. Outright persecution has a way of galvanizing people's convictions. The line is drawn in the sand. "Choose this day whom you will serve" (Josh. 24:15). The blood of the martyrs is the seed of the church.[29] But slow-acting social pressure is often more effective at wearing down convictions.

Thus, as Kierkegaard observes, "in the old days people were thrown to wild beasts," but in the modern world they are thrown to the public by way of the press.[30] As a result, "if Christ came to the world now, he would perhaps not be put to death, but would be ridiculed. This is martyrdom in the age of reason."[31] Similarly, "in the age of reason, 'ridicule' is the most feared of all dangers; in our times a person can more easily bear everything but being made a laughingstock, not to mention being exposed to daily ridicule—people shrink more from this danger than from the most torture-filled death."[32]

This kind of social opposition is especially difficult for Christians who have made a priority of cultural relevance and presenting the gospel in a seeker-friendly way. We assume that if we could just find the right way to present the gospel, people would accept it. And if people just got to know us, they would see we're really not so bad after all.

There is merit to the strategy of cultural engagement and relevance. But we should not be overconfident in it. At some point every genuine encounter with the gospel will run into the stumbling block of the cross. And the world does not want the cross, regardless of how attractive and relevant our presentation of the gospel. Ultimately one must choose between the way of the world and the way of the cross. You can't have it both ways.

It is good to seek common ground in cultural dialogue. This is what Paul did when he was addressing the philosophers in Athens (Acts 17:22–32). Mars Hill has thus come to represent intellectual and cultural engagement. The church has done this in dialogue with both conservatives and progressives: "You like order and traditional values? Christianity has something to say about that! You like social justice? Christianity has something to say about that!"

There is nothing intrinsically wrong with this strategy of cultural relevance, but there is a danger of trying to minimize the offense, to cover over the call to deny oneself, take up the cross, and follow Jesus. The cross will offend in different ways in different places and times, but in the end it will offend. One writer captured this point particularly well: "If I profess, with the loudest voice and the clearest exposition, every portion of the truth of God except precisely that little point which the world and the devil are at that moment attacking, I am not confessing Christ…. Where the battle rages the loyalty of the soldier is proved."[33]

Jesus warns us that the world will hate us but only because it first hated him (John 15:18), and John teaches that we should not be surprised if the world hates Christians (1 John 3:13). But it must be said, this hatred and suffering should not be the result of actual wrongdoing or foolishness. It is hardly persecution to face justice for being a criminal or to have people annoyed with you for being obnoxious (1 Pet. 4:15). Don't be antagonistic. Don't develop a martyr complex either. Don't be surprised, but be prepared.

And most of all, rejoice!

Rejoice?

REJOICE IN SUFFERING

Suffering will come. It is inevitable. Yet Scripture commands us to rejoice in suffering. Peter tells us to expect trials and to be glad when they come (1 Pet. 4:12–13). Why should we rejoice? So that we "may also rejoice and be glad when his glory is revealed. If you are insulted for the name of Christ, you are blessed, because the Spirit of glory and of God rests upon you" (vv. 13–14). Peter assures his readers that by sharing in Christ's suffering, they also would share in "the glory that is going to be revealed" (5:1).

This idea of sharing in suffering—becoming participants or partakers in it—is essential to the Bible's view of suffering, that in fact, suffering is intrinsic to knowing the God who suffered. The cross not only shows us God's solidarity with us in our suffering; the cross also guarantees that we can only come to know the true God—the God who was crucified and the God who still has scars—through sharing in Christ's sufferings. If we want to know Christ and the power of his resurrected life, then we must share in his sufferings (Phil. 3:10).[34] Suffering moves us closer to the heart of God because suffering exists in the heart of God (Rev. 5:6).

But our experience of suffering can be isolating. We can feel alone when we suffer, even forsaken. Everyone else seems to be okay but us. But suffering can also lead us out of ourselves into relation with others and with God. The fellowship of suffering is not only with Christ but can also be with one another.

We see this in 2 Corinthians, where Paul writes of the way God comforts us in our afflictions—a comfort we can in turn share with others (1:3–4). There is a communion of suffering, in which we partake in the suffering of Christ and in the suffering of his body, the church (vv. 5–7). Both of these points are a source of encouragement, showing that in Christ there is no solitary suffering. We are in it together (1 Cor. 12:26; 2 Tim. 1:8; 2:3). This is why Peter encourages his readers, "Resist [the Devil], firm in your faith, knowing that the same kinds of suffering are being experienced by your brotherhood throughout the world" (1 Pet. 5:9).

This is easy to say but difficult to do. Suffering is difficult. It is hard to square with the way we envision the good life. Few of us would voluntarily choose suffering, nor should we; the way of the cross is not one of seeking out suffering, nor does it treat suffering as an end in itself. But suffering, when it comes, is the unavoidable way to new—and true—life.

When we are in Christ, our suffering is both transformed and transformative. Christ sets the enduring pattern—there is no new life without passing through the crucifixion. He has already blazed the trail for us: it is a suffering unto new life and a glory that is yet to be revealed in its fullness. Thus, Peter writes, "After you have suffered a little while, the God of all grace, who has called you to his eternal glory in Christ, will himself restore, confirm, strengthen, and establish you" (1 Pet. 5:10). This is our source of hope, happiness, and even rejoicing.

This is a joy that suffering cannot take from you, simply because it cannot take Christ from you. In fact, if you are patient, if you will let it, God can use this difficult season, to teach you to draw deeper and deeper from the true well of joy: God's own heart.

This joy is the focus of our next chapter.

CRUCIFORM GLORY

The End Is Joy

It is a Christian duty, as you know, for everyone to be as happy as he can.

C. S. Lewis

Perhaps you've been waiting for this chapter to arrive, wondering, *When am I going to get to the good news?* We've said the cruciform life is God's way to the good and beautiful life, but it may not feel good and beautiful. Maybe you're not convinced.

It can be confusing. If the cross means suffering and dying to ourselves and the world, then doesn't the cruciform life move us away from happiness? Isn't it even hostile to most of the things we enjoy in life?

In the Bible God calls us—indeed, *commands* us—to love and enjoy his good gifts in this life (Eccl. 9:7). We are commanded to rejoice in God (Ps. 32:11; Phil. 4:4). We are called to "suffer for his sake" (Phil. 1:29, see also Rom. 8:17). How can these two calls—to the cross and to joy—be heard in unison and be joined in harmony?

There is a temptation to misunderstand the cruciform life as one in which joy is deferred to the next life when we will see the beauty and glory of God face-to-face. And while it is true that the infinite bliss of our communion with God will swallow up the pain and suffering of our mortal lives (Rom. 8:18; 2 Cor. 5:4), at the same time, we are commanded both to take up our cross *and* be joyful in this life. We tend to think it must be one or the other. But God *commands* us to be joyful, not merely in the next life when we're safe and sound. But even now—in this life.[1]

We'll see in this chapter how our future hope, rather than simply negating our ordinary life in the world, actually sets us free to cheerfully enjoy the good gifts of God in this life. In fact, the Christian story is one in which the ordinary is never merely ordinary. Jesus entered into the ordinary, taking it up and transforming it through himself.

In Christ nothing and no one is lost. Instead, in Christ all ordinary things and persons receive their true meaning and worth. "The world *is* charged with the grandeur of God."[2] But how do we inhabit this glorious vision? But how do we hold together in harmony the call to the cross and the duty of delight?

We will offer four thoughts about how to do this. But first, we need to address a common argument against the cruciform understanding of joy.

NIETZSCHE ON SUFFERING AND THE JOYFUL YES TO LIFE

Does the good news of Jesus' death and resurrection amount to a denial of this life, with all our hope being invested in the next one? That is certainly how Nietzsche interprets Christianity. In his view Christianity teaches a hatred of this life; it's just a consolation for those not strong enough to cope with the hardships, disappointments, and suffering of life.

This is an essential point for Nietzsche: all human beings suffer. His question is, what is the goal, the purpose, the meaning of suffering?

If the human being believes his suffering is meaningful, then "he *wants* it, even seeks it out."[3] As Nietzsche says, "He who has a *why* to live for can bear almost any *how*."[4] But if a person believes his suffering is meaningless, this eventually leads to a "suicidal nihilism."[5] The will is ready to give up. Thus, a sense of meaning saves the will by giving it purpose.

And that is how Nietzsche sees Christianity giving people a reason to go on. Nietzsche understands Christianity as teaching that all our suffering in this life will find compensation in the next life, and therefore offering an ascetic ideal of self-denial. Nietzsche says this ideal expresses a "disgust with the senses, with reason itself … [as well as a] fear of happiness and beauty … [and a] desire to get away from all semblance, change, becoming, death, wish, desire itself."[6]

Nietzsche believes Christianity cannot accept life and the world as it is—filled with suffering and struggle—so instead it imagines another world and places all its hope for meaning and joy there. In his words, "The Christian denies even the happiest lot on earth: he is sufficiently weak, poor, disinherited to suffer from life in whatever form he meets it. The god on the cross is a curse on life, a signpost to seek redemption from life."[7]

By Nietzsche's interpretation, Christianity is profoundly nihilistic. It teaches a hatred of life, the body, and the physical world. It denies this life in favor of an imaginary, eternal afterlife.

One of the main goals of Nietzsche's philosophy is to overcome Christianity—and every other form of nihilism he perceived—in order to find real joy in this life. Instead of saying no to life, the body, and the world, Nietzsche wanted to proclaim a joyous yes. He wanted a celebration, a dance of life in this world—even in the midst of suffering. Nietzsche was a man closely acquainted with suffering, but instead of seeking to escape it, he wanted to embrace it and affirm life even at its worst.

NIETZSCHE AS A CRITIC OF THE CRUCIFORM LIFE

Nietzsche presents a significant objection to the cruciform life as the good life. In order to address his challenge, we should begin by pointing out that he makes a major assumption that there is no resurrection, no coming kingdom of God, and no new heaven and new earth. But what if the Christian story is true? By refusing the promise of God's healing of the world, the resurrection of the flesh and the restoration of all things, Nietzsche ultimately chose a mode of defiant despair that refused hope and the promise of true joy because he found them deeply offensive.

We might also point out that Nietzsche's description of Christianity is a caricature. Does it resemble any Christians you know? Most Western Christians seem to be pretty comfortable and seem to enjoy life. But that response doesn't go far enough, because Nietzsche could argue that this is only because those Christians are worldly and not taking the cross seriously.

The deepest challenge before us is to show why Nietzsche's interpretation of the cross is a misinterpretation. The answer to this challenge lies at the heart of the Christian conception of the good life. Because while Christians might be loath to admit they agree with Nietzsche, many seem to accept his basic premise that taking up our cross and choosing joy can't coexist. And we must therefore choose between them. The theology of glory always tempts us away from the cross and whispers that we can have the life God wants for us without having to go by way of the cross (Mark 8:32).

The cross does indeed pronounce a real no, but this no is for the sake of the true yes. The cross most definitely means dying to ourselves and the world, but the point is not to simply die. The point is that this death is the path to abundant life, to real joy. The no is for the sake of the yes, for the genuinely joyful life.

The end is joy, not only in the sense that joy will come at the end of the story but also in the sense that joy is the purpose of the call and commands Jesus gives us now.

The cruciform life is the opposite of a bait and switch. A bait and switch promises something good but delivers something much less. The cruciform life presents something hard and demanding—deny yourself, take up your cross—but delivers something amazing: it infuses even ordinary life with significance and joy. The call to the cross is a call to joy.

This is the paradox of the cruciform life. Our end is happiness, flourishing, joy. But if you pursue happiness as your primary goal, it will forever elude you. It is only when you die to the pursuit of your own happiness and surrender your claim to it that you receive it back—as a gift. Seek God—not happiness.[8]

RECOGNIZE THE GOOD IN THE ORDINARY

No doubt Nietzsche's view is extreme, but it is not uncommon in our modern world. Many people hold a view something like his, even if they don't express it with such vitriol.

Indeed, Charles Taylor says this assumption defines our modern age. In his influential book *A Secular Age*, Taylor charts the rise of what he called "exclusive humanism"—that is, the idea that human flourishing is an end in itself, that we can pursue a full, abundant life without relation to God or any other transcendent ends. Taylor notes that this vision is unprecedented in history.[9] And while this shift is evident among those with no religious affiliation—the group sociologists call "nones"—it is just as evident among religious believers, who increasingly believe that God has set up the world so we can enjoy our lives and simply make the world a better place.

This also includes a suspicion of traditional Christian ideals of self-denial, self-sacrifice, and self-transcendence—and a decided reluctance to speak of sin. These notes are downplayed or erased altogether since they appear oppressive, even dangerous, and are presumed to distort or damage people's self-image. Instead of teaching people to love themselves, they lead to shame and self-contempt, the thinking goes.

This lowering of horizons is a departure from the traditional Christian story (Col. 3:1–3). It is also a departure from the ancient philosophical traditions. For most ancient philosophers, there was a fundamental difference between the pursuit of ordinary life (things like food, home, work, family, etc.) and the pursuit of the *good* life. Of course, the pursuit of ordinary life is important. You need to pay attention to these things because they provide the infrastructure for the good life. But for the ancients the good life was not really about these things.[10]

Most every philosophical school would have agreed with Jesus' teaching that "one's life does not consist in the abundance of his possessions" (Luke 12:15). For them the good life was a life devoted to higher activities like deliberating about and pursuing moral virtue, pursuing the common good through politics and law, and philosophically contemplating the order of reality.[11] For the ancients, contemplation (*theoria*) was superior to practice or doing (*praxis*). And this hierarchy endured throughout the Middle Ages and the Renaissance. This explains how the pursuit of religious or scholarly vocations (priest, monk, or nun) came to be seen as higher, more significant activities.

But something happened in the early modern era. This old hierarchy was leveled, and people started to promote ordinary life as valuable in itself and not subordinate to supposedly higher pursuits. As Taylor puts it, "the locus of the good life" shifted "from some special range of higher activities and place[d] it within 'life' itself."[12]

This shift has many positives, and, according to Taylor, one of the key influences in this shift was the Protestant Reformation. The Reformers argued that there are no special or privileged positions in relation to God. Religious vocations and spiritual exercises do nothing to elevate ourselves in relation to God because everyone is equal and entirely dependent on God's grace. Laypeople are therefore not second-class citizens in the kingdom of God, and they should not be so in the church either. There was no longer a clear division between sacred and secular vocations, but instead, the Reformers recognized the priesthood of all believers.[13]

As Taylor recognizes, the Reformers were not inventing new ideas when they sought to affirm the worth of everyday life. They saw themselves as returning to a more biblical understanding of the world as God's good creation (Gen. 1:31). God cares about physical things, as we can see in the incarnation, the resurrection, and the promise of a new heaven and earth. The material body and the physical world matter to God, and our work in this world becomes a means by which we can serve God and love other human beings. You don't need to retreat to a monastery to serve God; you can do it in every task God gives you in the world.

Dorothy Sayers gives a forceful statement of this view of work, insisting that the church has "forgotten that the secular vocation is sacred." The church should instead show that "every maker and worker is called to serve God *in* his profession or trade—not outside it." More pointedly, "the worker's first duty is to *serve the work.*"[14]

The Protestant view of work reflects a positive, holistic vision of our worldly activities that we would do well to recover today, while always remembering that this interpretation is susceptible to two distinct dangers. First, it can lead to a secularization of Christianity—what Kierkegaard calls "Christendom," which is the unholy matrimony of the church and the world. "I can serve God in my secular vocation? Great!" But the danger arises when I suppose that simply doing my job *is* serving God, such that God calls me to nothing higher than being a good citizen, employee, and family man.[15]

The second danger is that the practical may crowd out all place for contemplation. Consider our love affair with the word *practical*, our desire to "make things practical," and our aversion to being seen as theoretical.

It is good to be productive, to do good things, and to order the world. But this becomes dangerous when activity becomes busyness, when results become the standard by which we measure the worth of our activities, when we justify ourselves by what we do, and when we no longer hear God's command to remember the Sabbath and keep it holy (Ex. 20:8). We were created for activity and rest—to be productive and fruitful and also to be still and silent, to behold the wonder and majesty of God's glory. We were made to enjoy communion with God.

This is the picture that philosophers, theologians, poets, and artists have drawn to describe true human flourishing: contemplation of the divine (Aristotle) and ultimately union with God (Plato). The Bible tells us it means we will see God face-to-face, knowing and being known by him (1 Cor. 8:3; 13:12; Gal. 4:9).

Our best theologians have insisted that human good is fulfilled in the *visio Dei*, the vision of the divine essence, the beatific vision—the blessed, blissful vision in which our nature as human beings is fulfilled as we participate in the divine nature—"we shall be like him, because we shall see him as he is" (1 John 3:2). Our ultimate enjoyment, our ultimate *joy*, lies in God.

But without combining this vision with a robust sense of how much the material world matters to God, this vision of eternal life can sound boring. It can sound like a never-ending church service. This misconception of heaven creates a problem for how we view our present life. It might seem as if the cruciform life is one of suffering and religious observation while we wait for joy. A life marked by the denial of self and world could seem to be pretty dreary—all flat and gray rather than vibrant with all the colors of creation. Joy is the end, but does God intend joy to be an essential part of the journey, even a duty? Another way to ask that question could be, *How do we inhabit the world of time when our end is in eternity?*

INHABIT TIME IN BIBLICAL WAYS

Charles Taylor argues that one of the formative features of our modern, secular age is the flattening, or leveling, of time.[16] In the premodern world there was a distinction between different times. Festivals and holidays—*holy days*—stood out from regular times. The same is true of the Sabbath.

For us, increasingly, there is no qualitative distinction between different times. Time is an empty, neutral container. Every day is just another day. This is particularly true in the United States. Every day, every hour, is a time to work, to buy, to sell, to consume. Everything is available all the time. At first this feels liberating—no need to wait—but it's really enslaving because it gives no rest. No genuine leisure. No time or space to be still and know that God is God (Ps. 46:10).[17]

One of the consequences of this view of time is it makes it harder for us to recognize the seasons of life. The book of Ecclesiastes reminds us of these seasons:

> For everything there is a season, and a time for
> every matter under heaven:
>> a time to be born, and a time to die;
>> a time to plant, and a time to pluck up what
> is planted;
>> a time to kill, and a time to heal;
>> a time to break down, and a time to build up;
>> a time to weep, and a time to laugh;

> a time to mourn, and a time to dance;
>
> a time to cast away stones, and a time to gather stones together;
>
> a time to embrace, and a time to refrain from embracing;
>
> a time to seek, and a time to lose;
>
> a time to keep, and a time to cast away;
>
> a time to tear, and a time to sew;
>
> a time to keep silence, and a time to speak;
>
> a time to love, and a time to hate;
>
> a time for war, and a time for peace. (3:1–8)

This passage is instructive because it challenges the idea that time is a neutral, empty container that we can fill with whatever projects we happen to desire at the moment. On the contrary, it teaches that there are qualitatively different seasons in life.

If Ecclesiastes challenges our secularization of time, it also challenges a kind of *religious* idea of time that is similarly flat and homogeneous. A certain religious zeal might imagine that the cruciform life is all about one mode of time: that every day, every hour, should be devoted to some sort of religious observation. What justification is there for doing anything else, like watching a baseball game, when you could spend that time praying, reading the Bible, or serving the poor? Ecclesiastes shows there are different times with different activities.

This point really comes home, however, when we consider the life of Jesus. Jesus took time to grow in the womb of Mary.

He lived a full childhood and learned the art of carpentry from his father—a job he pursued for years before beginning his public ministry. It's important to notice that Jesus did not simply show up and start his ministry—a ministry that took up only one-tenth of the time that his preceding life did. And during that ministry Jesus showed what it looks like to inhabit fully the different seasons of life: a time to attend weddings and a time for mourning; a time to feast and a time to fast; a time to teach crowds and a time to withdraw into solitude for spiritual renewal. In Jesus' life, there was a time to speak words of grace and mercy, and a time to speak of divine judgment.

As the Teacher in Ecclesiastes writes, "He has made everything beautiful in its time" (3:11). These different times are to be received as gifts from God. The Teacher continues, writing that God has also "put eternity into man's heart" (v. 11). This means that no moment of time, no finite pleasure, is enough to satisfy our longing for the eternal. This profound insight gives us the interpretive key for understanding the right relation between loving God and enjoying his gifts.

ENJOY THE GIFTS OF GOD (A FULL-BLOWN WORLDLINESS)

Other passages from Ecclesiastes help us here. More than once the Teacher writes that eating, drinking, working—as well as wealth and possessions—are gifts from God to human beings (2:24; 3:12–13; 5:18–20; 8:15). As God's gifts they are to be enjoyed.

So the Teacher writes, "Go, eat your bread with joy, and drink your wine with a merry heart, for God has already approved what you do" (9:7). We do not need additional justification to enjoy the good gifts of God. These are good things created by God, and they are not to be treated as evil. Augustine writes this in a brief fragment of poetry:

> These things are Yours, O God. They
> are good, because You created them.
> None of our evil is in them. The
> evil is ours if we love them
> At the expense of Yourself—these
> things that reflect Your design.[18]

Augustine's stipulation agrees with the Teacher in Ecclesiastes: these created goods become corrupted or meaningless only when we pursue them instead of God. These gifts are from the hands of God, "for apart from him … who can have enjoyment?" (2:25). "Apart from [God]"—there are two levels of meaning in this phrase: first, God is the giver, and without him we would have nothing; second, if we try to take these gifts to the exlusion of the giver, they become meaningless.

Augustine gives a great illustration of this point. Imagine, he writes, a man who makes a ring for his fiancé. Naturally she would be delighted by the gift. But imagine further that she loves the ring more than the fiancé who gave it to her and that she decides, "The ring is enough. I do not want to see his face again." Cut off from the relationship to her fiancé, the ring loses its meaning and starts to seem absurd. It is entirely fitting that she love the ring, but her fiancé gave it to her so that "he himself may be loved." The analogy is clear: God has given us all these good things, but like the ring they are meant to point beyond themselves to the giver. The right way to enjoy these gifts is to love the God who gives them.[19]

All too often, though, we seek our ultimate enjoyment in created things rather than in the Creator. But this is a request no finite thing can fulfill, a demand no finite thing can meet. We are asking too much of finite things. So the gift goes bad. The fruit of life turns sour. Vanity, vanity—all is vanity (Eccl. 1:2).

The things that we enjoy are supposed to point beyond themselves. George Herbert describes this in his poem "The Pulley":

> When God at first made man,
> Having a glass of blessings standing by,
> Let us (said he) pour on him all we can:
> Let the world's riches, which dispersèd lie,
> Contract into a span.
>
> So strength first made a way;
> Then beauty flow'd, then
> wisdom, honour, pleasure:
> When almost all was out, God made a stay,
> Perceiving that alone of all his treasure
> Rest in the bottom lay.

> For if I should (said he)
> Bestow this jewel also on my creature,
> He would adore my gifts instead of me,
> And rest in Nature, not the God of Nature:
> So both should losers be.
>
> Yet let him keep the rest,
> But keep them with repining restlessness:
> Let him be rich and weary, that at least,
> If goodness lead him not, yet weariness
> May toss him to my breast.[20]

This is a reflection of Augustine's point that our hearts are restless until they rest in God.[21] That restlessness, that longing, comes from God having set eternity in our hearts. Nothing less will do.

When we love God rightly, then the rest of our loves fall into place. The key to happiness and the good life is that our loves are rightly ordered. We love God's gifts rightly when we love them in God. Once we see created things as from God, they are set free to be what they are: not substitutes for God but rather gifts that are good and to be enjoyed in their proper seasons.

Bonhoeffer describes this plurality of seasons in terms of "the polyphony of life." Human existence is made up of multiple harmonies, and the good news does not reduce these to a flat, monotonous drone. God is like the *cantus firmus*, the fixed melody that provides the basis for all the other melodies to work together in harmony. Bonhoeffer writes, "God, the Eternal, wants to be loved with our whole heart, not to the detriment of earthly love or to diminish it, but as a sort of cantus firmus to which the other voices of life resound in counterpoint.... Where the cantus firmus is clear and distinct, a counterpoint can develop as mightily as it wants.... Only this polyphony gives your life wholeness."[22]

With God as the fixed basis for our life, the other melodies are not threatened but are set in tune and become more harmonious. This allows us to delight in the plurality, to receive it as a gift. Bonhoeffer writes in another letter,

> One should find and love God in what God directly gives us; if it pleases God to allow us to enjoy an overwhelming earthly happiness, then *one shouldn't be more pious than God* and allow this happiness to be gnawed away through arrogant thoughts and challenges and wild religious fantasy that is never satisfied with what God gives. God will not fail the person who finds his earthly happiness in God and is grateful, in those hours when he is reminded that all earthly things are temporary and that it is good to accustom his heart to eternity, and finally the hours will not fail to come in which we can honestly say, "I wish that I were home."[23]

Bonhoeffer's point is that we should not rush ahead to this wish and cultivate a contempt or hatred of what God has given to us: the people he has given us to love, the things and the work he has given us to do, and the blessings he has given us to enjoy. When we receive the world as a gift, we can inhabit the world with what Bonhoeffer calls a "genuine and full-blown worldliness."[24]

REMEMBER THAT YOU MATTER

The little things matter. The mundane material of our ordinary, everyday lives matters to God. He is concerned with not only the so-called religious aspects of our lives, because the entire business of our lives as human beings in the world is part of God's good creation. When our loves are rightly ordered, all of this is part of glorifying and enjoying God.

The fact that little things matter to God is central to our hope and the promise of eternal happiness. It was also a radical innovation in the ancient world. It is one more feature of the scandal of the cross. Little things—and little people—matter to God.

We see this in the story of Peter's denial of Jesus. Peter was an intense man. He was the one who vowed he would never deny Jesus, even if he had to die with him (Mark 14:31). He was the one who took a sword and cut off the ear of the high priest's servant when the soldiers came for Jesus in the garden (John 18:10). He was ready to fight. He was the one who was brave enough to hang around outside while Jesus was being questioned (vv. 15–16). But when someone suggested that he knew Jesus, Peter denied it. Angrily. And he denied him three times, just as Jesus had predicted (Mark 14:66–71). Peter realized this when he heard the rooster crow, and he started to weep (v. 72).

The literary critic Erich Auerbach points out that this story is unprecedented among the literature of ancient Greece and Rome, which was typically concerned with the words and deeds of the nobility. If slaves or commoners showed up, it was usually in the interest of a farce or comedy. But here the text takes Peter's grief seriously and depicts it with sympathy. Here we see experiences of common people in everyday life assuming an importance that was never conveyed by ancient poets or historians.[25]

Christianity tells a story in which the small, the common, the mundane are meaningful. This is where God chooses to work.

The American novelist Walker Percy argues that this is why "the novel is a creature of the Christian West"—because it shows something "happening in ordinary time to ordinary people, not to epic heroes in mythic time." Christianity is a story that "awards an absolute importance to an Event which happened to a Person in historic time.... Judeo-Christianity is about pilgrims who have something wrong with them and are embarked on a search to find a way out. This is also what novels are about."[26]

Apart from the Christian story, it seems presumptuous to think that these little stories about ordinary people in ordinary circumstances matter or would be of interest to anyone but those involved.[27] Yet this is what the Christian story does. It gives permission to this presumption. God shows this concern with the ordinary by entering into it. The extraordinary entered the ordinary.

This offends aristocratic sensibilities. Nietzsche complains that the New Testament's concern with commoners is in bad taste:

"Their ambition is laughable: people of *that* sort regurgitating their most private affairs, their stupidities, sorrows, and petty worries, as if the Heart of Being were obliged to concern itself with them; they never grow tired of involving God himself in even the pettiest troubles they have got themselves into. And the appalling taste of this perpetual familiarity with God."[28]

Nietzsche finds this familiarity overwhelmingly gauche, but this is the heart of the Christian story. God made himself familiar by becoming human.

The eternal Word was born in a manger. He grew up in Nazareth. "Can anything good come out of Nazareth?" (John 1:46). He spent the first thirty years of his life in relative anonymity, and his public ministry lasted a mere three years. He became well known in Jewish circles but was relatively unnoticed by his Roman overlords, who ended up being talked into crucifying him—a death contrived to eliminate enemies of Rome from memory. How many thousands of people were crucified and abandoned by the Romans? Yet this death became central to God's salvation of the world. The cross and resurrection is Jesus' victory over death.

The Gospels contain several episodes in which Jesus brought back someone from the dead. With the exception of Lazarus (John 11:43–44), none are named. Yet Jesus was deeply affected when he heard of the deaths of these particular people, for them and for those in mourning. He "saw" them and "had compassion" for them and moved toward them (Luke 7:11–17).

As Romano Guardini observes, "Jesus is touched by some human fate. A human sorrow presents itself to him: sorrow of a mother, a father, bereaved sisters, confronting him with the image of an existence uprooted and flung into the inexplicableness of death." Jesus is "profoundly shaken" by the deaths, and in these moments "he seems to step into the fate of the individual, ordering the events of the world from the inside. For one instant created by the Savior's love, a human heart forms the decisive center of world reality."[29]

From the perspective of the universe as a whole, with its vast expanse of space and its stars and planets, what is the worth of this one person? But these miracles of healing and return from death show a different perspective—"the world as it appears to God: the world viewed from within, from the perspective of the human heart and human fate."[30] These particular human sufferings and griefs matter to God. Not only did Jesus overcome death, but he also overcame the anonymity of death. This is a key feature of the good news of the Christian story. We want to know that we matter, that we will be remembered.

WHO WILL REMEMBER YOU?

This desire to be remembered is at the center of the Pixar movie *Coco*.[31] It is set around Día de los Muertos, the Mexican festival called Day of the Dead. Families remember, honor, and pray for loved ones who have died. The premise of the story is that these memories keep the departed in existence in the Land of the Dead. When people are forgotten, they disappear.

The hero of the story, young Miguel, is an aspiring musician who accidentally ends up in the Land of the Dead and is trying to get back home. Miguel meets his great-great-grandfather, who helps him return home, and also gains his great-great-grandmother's approval to pursue his love of music. It's a beautiful story of love, family, and tradition, and the grand finale is a soaring anthem in which Miguel sings that his love for his ancestors will live on forever in every beat of his heart.

It's a beautiful song and a beautiful sentiment. It attests to the desire to be remembered. And it would be nice to think that it's true. But we know it can't be—their love can't live on forever if it depends on Miguel, for his heart will evenutally stop beating. After a few generations, all of us will be forgotten. In the memory of this world, most everyone's destiny is oblivion.

The good news that we might tell Miguel is that God has a story even better than Miguel's: the story of the cross and resurrection. In Christ no one is forgotten. Generations may pass and memories may fade, but God remembers us all. This is a God who notices every sparrow that falls (Matt. 10:29). God sends rain to nourish grass that no human being will ever see (Job 38:25–27).[32] If this is how God cares for plants and animals, how much more does he care for human beings (Matt. 6:25–31)?

Even the criminal executed by Rome asked Jesus to remember him when Jesus came into his kingdom (Luke 23:42). Who still knows this man's name? We may not, but Jesus does, because he promised him, "Truly, I say to you, today you will be with me in paradise" (v. 43). A criminal designated for annihilation by the Roman Empire is remembered by Jesus in the kingdom. Truly no human being is faceless. No human being is anonymous. No one is forgotten. All are remembered. There are no invisible people with God.

This is the privilege of our union with Christ. Through him God has adopted us as his children, and because we are in Christ, we are redeemed by his blood and our sins are forgiven "according to the riches of his grace, which he lavished upon us, in all wisdom and insight making known to us the mystery of his will, according to his purpose, which he set forth in Christ as a plan for the fullness of time, to unite all things in him, things in heaven and things on earth" (Eph. 1:5–10).

Pay attention to that last bit: God has promised that, in the fullness of time, all things in heaven and on earth will be united in Christ. The Greek word here means that in Christ all creation is gathered together and summed up under his headship.[33] In him all creation is *recapitulated*, and this will be fully manifest in the fullness of time. This is grand stuff indeed!

This was an important theme among the church fathers, most notably Irenaeus[34] and later Maximus the Confessor.[35] Bonhoeffer calls this doctrine of recapitulation "a magnificent and consummately consoling thought." It is the thought that in this grand story "nothing is lost; in Christ all things are taken up, preserved, albeit in transfigured form, transparent, clear, liberated from the torment of self-serving demands. Christ brings all this back, indeed, as God intended, without being distorted by sin."[36]

This is the culmination of the cosmic symphony, the grand story of how God redeems, restores, and brings his creation into the fullness of its glory. A glory that comes by way of the cross. A glory that comes by way of shame, rejection, suffering, and death. This is our destiny, and this is why C. S. Lewis famously writes, "There are no *ordinary* people."[37] But there are no ordinary birds or dogs either!

One day the mountains will sing and the trees will clap (Isa. 55:12). This is the glory that we were created for: to know God, to experience the true flourishing of ourselves and all creation in communion with God. And through him, to know the rest of creation as it was meant to be known. This will be true with our friends and our neighbors and even our enemies. Peace and reconciliation are made possible through his cross. This is even true of the world of animals. The lion will lie down with the calf (Isa. 11:6). The entire chain of being is rightly ordered in relation to its creator.

Nothing is lost. No note in the symphony is incidental or accidental. No face is forgotten. He will be all in all (1 Cor. 15:28). Every tear will be wiped away (Rev. 21:4). It's the certainty of the world's end (and new beginning) that makes joy possible, even obligatory, until we see him in whose "presence there is fullness of joy" (Ps. 16:11).

CRUCIFORM LIVING

A Theology of the Cross for Daily Life

There was a day when I died, utterly died, died to George Müller, his opinions, preferences, tastes and will—died to the world, its approval or censure—died to the approval or blame even of my brethren and friends—and since then I have studied only to show myself approved unto God.

George Müller, *George Müller of Bristol*

The greatest burden we have to carry in life is self. The most difficult thing we have to manage is self.... In laying off your burdens, therefore, the first one you must get rid of is yourself. You must hand yourself ... over into the care and keeping of your God.... He made you, and therefore He understands you, and knows how to manage you; and you must trust Him to do it.

Hannah Whitall Smith, *The Christian's Secret of a Happy Life*

Let's return to the basic thesis of this book. *Happiness is communion with God. And the way to that communion is the way of the cross.*

The more you tease out the implications, the more it dawns on you how this could affect the most mundane choices and practical details of your everyday life. In fact, that's where the battle must be fought—in the trenches of our daily rituals and routines.

Not only does Jesus show us who God is; Jesus also shows us who we are. He reveals to us—all of us, regardless of our background or beliefs, regardless of what we think of Jesus—what we were made for. "Who is this Jesus?" a street vendor asked Rankin through an interpreter in a small village in southwest China. Jesus shows everyone created in God's image what a fully human life looks like. Jesus reveals who humanity was created to be and who we were redeemed to become. And yet he also shows that the shape of this life is not what we were expecting.

"Realize that you must lead a dying life; the more a man dies to himself, the more he begins to live unto God," writes Thomas à Kempis.[1] And precisely this—communion with the living God—is the true, full life we are all seeking.

We opened this book by showing that each one of us is interested in human flourishing. Our argument throughout has been that Jesus' way is *the* way to the abundant life that God intends for the creatures he made. Christianity is eminently practical. It does lead to the life you've always wanted—just not in the way you ever expected. God is supremely good, and he designed the world so that what brings him the most glory brings his creatures the fullest satisfaction and deepest joy.

But "the word of the cross" has always been and always will be a scandal, a stumbling block, an offense, to our understanding of things (1 Cor. 1:18). Jesus walked the way of humility, service, self-sacrifice, and suffering, the way of self-denial, the way of placing others' interests above his own, the way of costly love, the way of grace, the way of the cross. The end is joy and peace and—*and, not but!*—the way is the cross.

In this sense, self-denial has been said to be the essence of the Christian life, the first lesson in Christ's school. The cross is God's wisdom for salvation, and one of the most basic definitions of the New Testament word for "save" is *heal.* If we would be healed (John 5:6), this is God's way, the way of the cross. Not simply once and for all but as a way of life. We must adopt a continuing posture of complete surrender to God's will in every circumstance. The cross teaches us a new way of life, a new habit of being, one of dying to our comfort and our control. We have "a self to lose and a self to find."[2] To use Paul's words it is the "old self" that we must deny. The way of "I am what I do and I am what I have" must be cracked open, fall into the earth, and die (John 12:24).

Our lives are not our own. We must die to our plans and our sense of what makes for a successful life. We must die to our own vision of the good and beautiful life. We must die to our expectations of the life that we thought God was supposed to give us if we did the things that we thought God was asking us to do. We must die to our reputation and let the word of Christ be our reputation. We must die to our own "immortality projects." We must die to getting our own way. We must die as a way of life—that's the cruciform way.[3]

The cruciform way is God's way to the good and beautiful life. The cruciform path is God's wisdom for navigating the complexities of life.

Ah, but we don't think so. It's so hard for us to believe Jesus' way is the way to life ... because it feels like death. God's call is so countercultural in an upwardly mobile world. It makes no sense in our day to believe that we can move up only by going down and deeper into the love of Jesus. The cross turns our vision of the world upside down—but in doing so, it turns things right side up. We must start over at the beginning and relearn everything (see Matt. 18:3 THE MESSAGE).

This chapter gets at a question that has been looming over the whole book: *How?*

Even if you accept that Jesus' call to take up your cross and follow him (Luke 9:23) is an invitation to a full and free life, how does that get lived out? How do we move that from a provocative idea to a transformative habit?

What does the cruciform life look like lived? How does it become more and more a way of life and not just a paradoxical cliché? We've heard "the way up is the way down," "come and die that you may truly live," "lose your life to find your life," "strength through weakness," and "freedom through surrender." These wonderful paradoxes roll off our tongues but don't seem to settle into the marrow of our lives.

We can use Christian jargon as a defense mechanism to keep us from dying to ourselves. We talk about the cross, but perhaps only so as to keep ourselves from having to live a dying life. What is the domino that must fall for the cruciform life to become a daily pursuit?

THE BEAUTY OF HOLINESS

The cruciform life will never be attractive to you unless holiness becomes beautiful to you. This requires a revolution in our imaginations so that we begin to see holiness—and happiness—anew.

You may have heard well-meaning preachers say, "God is concerned not with your happiness but with your holiness." There is some truth in that sentiment. Our personal well-being doesn't sit at the center of the gospel. Otherwise we make ourselves the center of the gospel, which is a recipe for resentment when our expectations are not met.

But if the cruciform life is God's blueprint for human flourishing, then holiness and happiness should not be pitted against each other as opposites. Because God loves us, he intends that we should be holy and happy—and happy only because we are holy. You'll never be happy in life with God until holiness becomes your treasure, because holiness is who God is.[4]

Jonathan Edwards wrote *Religious Affections*, which is considered to be one of the most important books ever penned on American soil. Edwards asserts that the distinguishing mark of genuine conversion is to apprehend the beauty of God's holiness.[5]

How do you know whether you have truly experienced God? How do you know, one might say, whether you are a real Christian? Writing in the midst of the Great Awakening, when a high premium was placed on religious experience, Edwards argues there is one distinguishing mark. All the other attributes of God—his power, his love, his wisdom, his compassion—benefit us. But Edwards says there is one attribute of God that does not benefit us directly but rather terrifies us when we first encounter it, and that is God's holiness.[6]

Only someone whose sin had been exposed by God's holy justice but then atoned for by God's holy love would come to see the beauty of God's holiness, would be drawn toward and not repelled by God's transcendent moral majesty, would begin to see that God saved us not merely from our sins but for holiness. "He died to make men holy," the old hymn puts it.[7]

Holiness is the great end of our redemption (Eph. 1:4). The biblical pattern is that God declared us holy so that we might become so. Union with Christ makes the pursuit of holiness a duty of delight as God takes us by the hand, as it were (Ps. 73:23), and says, "Child, become what you are." The gospel and only the gospel makes the call to become holy (1 Pet. 1:15) not burdensome (1 John 5:3) but a privilege.[8]

THE JOY OF COMMUNION

But the pursuit of holiness is a means to an even greater end. Personal transformation is the great promise of the gospel. You can change, and you will (2 Cor. 3:18). But personal transformation is not the goal. It's not the ultimate reward of those who seek God. The prize the apostle Paul is referring to when he exhorts his readers, like athletes in training, to "run in such a way as to get the prize" (1 Cor. 9:24 NIV) is not their own spiritual health.

The prize is communion with God. As J. I. Packer notes, "To the Puritans, communion between God and man is the end to which both creation and redemption are but the means; it is the goal to which both theology and preaching must ever point."⁹ Communion with God is our highest privilege and the hinge on which all true happiness turns. To say it more simply, if you don't enjoy God, if you don't long for his presence and yearn to gaze upon his beauty (Ps. 27:4), if the thought of seeing him and becoming like him is not the overriding passion in your life (1 Cor. 13:12; 1 John 3:2), then the call to cruciform living will sound only like a religious-sounding, pietistic killjoy. The way of the cross will seem like drudgery—something you know is good for you but something you don't really want.

Unless you "hunger and thirst for righteousness" (Matt. 5:6) and the communion it brings with the Righteous One, this call to cruciform living will never compel you, let alone be beautiful to you. The question "How does one die daily?" can be asked only after the questions "What do you want?" (Matt. 20:21) and "Do you want to be healed?" (John 5:6).

You must first become convinced that your old way of living does not work.

But God's mercy and grace open the eyes of our hearts and enable us to see that contentment is never going to come from getting what we thought we wanted. Ah, but what do you want? What were you made for? When the answer becomes "I want to be conformed to the image of Christ" (see Rom. 8:29) and "I want to be holy, for that is what I was made for" (see Eph. 4:24), then you are walking in a manner worthy of the gospel.

The gospel says that in Christ you have been completely and definitively accepted. You want to be holy—not so you can be accepted but because you have already been. You want to be holy so you can experience more and more communion with God (1 John 2:6). You want to be holy—not so you will be loved but because you want to *experience* the love of God more and more. You want to experience God's loving embrace. You want to know God more each day through obeying him more each day.

When the beauty of holiness and the joy of communion come together in your desire, then the call to cruciform living becomes a call to holiness *and* happiness. They become the same thing and are inseparable. Communion with God is the joy set before us and our very great reward.

ATTENDING TO WEEDS

Communion with the invisible God gets high-minded very quickly. How does this get brought down to earth so you can "walk in a manner worthy of the Lord" (Col. 1:10)?

The greatest threat to—and therefore the greatest opportunity for—living out the cruciform life is found not in the momentous or conspicuous decisions and not even in the cultivation of spiritual exercises, as important as they are. What can be even more important and formative are what Nietzsche (in another context, of course) calls the "small weeds."[10] These are the matters that are easily overlooked, especially by those who are keen to focus on the care of their souls. These are the things we do while "on our way." These spaces between our spiritual practices are often more critical and formative than those deliberative exercises themselves.

As I (Rankin) was working on this chapter, there was a man outside my office window, all decked out in exercise gear and on his way to the high-priced gym next door. And he was smoking a cigarette. Right before his workout. We smile in compassion because we recognize the contradiction. Nietzsche, who is the actual originator of the phrase "long obedience in the same direction,"[11] writes of the importance of the thousand tiny decisions that make up our days: "The little vegetation that grows in between everything and understands how to cling everywhere, this is what ruins what is great in us—the quotidian, hourly pitifulness of our environment that goes overlooked, the thousand tiny tendrils of this or that small and small-minded feeling growing out of our neighborhood, our job, the company we keep, the division of our day. If we allow these small weeds to grow unwittingly, then unwittingly they will destroy us!"[12]

The stuff of our lives—our daily discourse, the quotidian chores of picking up after ourselves, eating and drinking, driving, picking up the kids, greeting strangers, not to mention speaking to our own families—these should all become occasions for us to "wittingly" pull up the small weeds of selfishness and excessive self-concern. Otherwise these "thousand tiny tendrils" will strangle and overwhelm our most sincere efforts toward personal change and spiritual formation.

We tend to focus on our episodic or annual resolutions—pray more, read the Bible more, get up earlier, journal—forgetting that the small everyday things will help or harm us the most. The times between our focused moments of physical or soul care (usually while we are on our way or looking at our screens) have much more to do with who we are becoming.

We must be about pulling these invasive weeds, intentionally and daily (Luke 9:23), seeing this soul gardening not as a burden but as most essential if we would become (in Christ) who we want to be (like Christ). After all, as Annie Dillard puts it, "How we spend our days is ... how we spend our lives."[13]

CHOOSING THE LITTLE WAY

One of the best examples of living the cruciform life was Thérèse of Lisieux. Thérèse was born in 1873 in France into a devout and happy family. Her mom died when she was four, but Thérèse was a cheerful girl and drawn to God from a young age. "I loved God very much," she wrote later, "and offered my heart to Him very often."[14]

When she was nine, she decided that she wanted to be a nun, but she was impatient. She did not want to wait until she got older, so when she was fourteen, on a trip with her father to Rome, she personally petitioned the pope for special permission—such was her strength of will![15] She was what today we'd call a gifted child with a strong personality. Thérèse wanted to become a missionary to Vietnam and dreamed of doing great things for God. But she woke up one morning at the age of twenty-three to find that she had coughed up blood. She died a year later. Her brief life was marked by suffering.

During her illness she completed her spiritual autobiography, which has come to be known as *The Story of a Soul,* where she wrote about the "little way" to God. Thérèse had wanted to do *great things, big things,* but here she was dying. Moreover, she knew that she lacked the virtue of her saintly heroes. So she chose to receive the small hardships of daily life as tests of her devotion and, as such, gifts from God.

"I applied myself to practicing little virtues," she wrote, "not having the capability of practicing the great."[16] Thérèse would choose to sit beside the sisters she found most difficult to get along with, and she tried hardest to love the ones who were the least kind. "Because of my lack of virtue," she wrote, "these little practices cost me very much and I had to console myself with the thought that at the Last Judgment everything would be revealed."[17]

No one expected her little book to be read beyond her sisters, but to everyone's surprise it became one of the bestselling spiritual memoirs of the twentieth century. Her little way was one that normal people, not saintly heroes, could identify with. The little way—these tiny deaths, these secret mortifications, these small daily choices—can look like this:

- seeking out the menial job
- welcoming unjust criticisms
- befriending those who annoy us

- helping those who are ungrateful
- forgiving without condition
- overlooking an offense
- praying for your enemies

Anyone can choose the little way, and that happens to be the Way. Every day presents us with countless opportunities to walk in the little way. Jesus calls us to take up our cross daily and follow him with the promise, "Whoever would save his life will lose it, but whoever loses his life for my sake will save it" (Luke 9:23–24). "Dying to self is not a thing we do once for all. There may be an initial dying when God first shows these things, but ever after it will be a constant dying, for only so can the Lord Jesus be revealed constantly through us."[18]

Nothing could be further from our "selfie" moment than these calls to the little way, but nothing better captures the core of the cruciform life. We are not our own. We belong, body and soul, to God and to our faithful Savior, Jesus Christ, in life and in death.[19] If you want God's wisdom in any circumstance, always remember: the cross before me. That is the way forward.[20]

HABITS OF BEING: THE IMPORTANCE OF SPIRITUAL EXERCISES

Since Dallas Willard's *Spirit of the Disciplines* and Richard Foster's *Celebration of Discipline* were published, there has been a renewed interest in spiritual formation and the vital role that spiritual disciplines play in this pursuit. *The Cross Before Me* is not a book on spiritual disciplines, but we do wish to emphasize how necessary spiritual exercises are to spiritual health.

Living the cruciform life is simply not possible without cultivating new habits of being, and nothing imprints these new habits of being more deeply or consistently than spiritual exercises practiced routinely.

People can say they want to be physically fit. But if they pay little or no regard to what they eat and don't exercise, then it doesn't matter how much they talk about wanting to be healthy. If they do not avail themselves of what is necessary, then they do not really want to be healthy—not enough to make a change. Our habits are deeper than our convictions. In fact, our habits often reveal our deepest convictions.

It's the same with spiritual exercises (and we'll show in a moment why we prefer this phrase to the more palatable *spiritual disciplines* or *means of grace*). To be clear, the exercises by themselves do not change us, nor does our zeal in practicing them earn us any merit or favor with God. The grace of God is what changes us. But spiritual exercises are the means, the ordinary means, God has provided for his grace to flow into our lives. Spiritual exercises are channels for God's grace.

These aren't the only means of God's grace, but they are the primary means God has given us. Therefore, we believe that to not avail ourselves of these means (prayer, meditating on and memorizing God's Word, regularly worshipping in community, and taking the Lord's Supper, to name a few) is a sad admission that, despite what we say, we do not wish to be healed (John 5:6). As diet and exercise are inseparable from physical health, so spiritual exercises are inseparable from spiritual health. We must exercise, and we need to recover this old phrase: *spiritual exercises*.

Earlier we mentioned Pierre Hadot, who was a twentieth-century French philosopher. His work centers around showing that, for the ancients, philosophy was not a theoretical enterprise but a way of life, an art of living. For the ancient Greeks and Romans, living a philosophical life entailed a conversion, a decisive break with an old way and entering into a new form of life, typically by belonging to a group or school or community.

A vital part of this new form of life was the practice of "spiritual exercises," which Hadot defines as "voluntary, personal practices" intended to transform the self and its ways of seeing, being, and acting.[21] These practices were called "exercises" because they were very similar to the exercise (*askesis*) of athletes, with whom philosophers often shared gymnasiums. The classroom and the workout room were often the same room.

Just as these athletes pursued physical health and strove for peak physical form, so the budding philosophy student pursued the ideals of self-mastery and spiritual health. Most of the philosophical schools had exercises in common: meditation, memorization, contemplation, dialogue, and reading, almost always under the guidance of a teacher or mentor. The goal was personal education (the Greek word was *paideia*), but this education was more about personal transformation than just imparting information. It was aimed at the formation of virtue, which they believed was the necessary condition of happiness.[22]

The disciple was rigorously trained to no longer live in conformity with his old patterns. Truth was meant to be lived, not merely understood. What these philosophers saw—and what we miss today—is that this truth may be reached and internalized only through practice, through exercise, through discipline.[23]

Certain branches of the church today have missed this. Somehow it has become fixed in our minds that grace is opposed to effort or striving, so the call to exercise, to "work out your salvation" (Phil. 2:12), can come across as diminishing the great gospel promise that we are made right with God by grace alone through faith alone apart from any works on our behalf.[24]

And it is very easy for a theology of the cross, which calls us to die to ourselves every day, to slip into a theology of glory, a self-righteous way that is self-focused and centers on our own virtue and therefore serves only to inflate our own pride: "Look at me, the truly devoted, the truly disciplined one. Not like other people" (see Luke 18:11).

Those of us in the Reformed church, in particular, need to recover our heritage. Martin Luther and John Calvin decried the misuses of monasticism and the abuses of asceticism. They advocated the priesthood of all believers. But what they were railing against was not personal devotion but the very notion of a two-tiered church: on the one hand, the serious and devout clergy who had ostensibly given their whole lives over to God and, on the other hand, the lukewarm laity who could leave the serious work of whole-life consecration to the priests and nuns.

In his book *Life in God*, Matthew Myer Boulton shows that the Protestant Reformers, while extremely critical of monasticism, were nonetheless zealous advocates of spiritual exercises for all Christians.[25] The priesthood of all believers dignified the value of ordinary, nonclerical work. At the same time, it called the cobbler or the blacksmith to be just as disciplined in spiritual devotion as any priest ever was. Everyone—not just the priests and nuns but every follower of Jesus—was to have a daily rule of life ordered around prayer, work, and God's Word.

For the cruciform life to become our way of life, we must recover the ancient wisdom of the necessity of spiritual exercises for spiritual health and transformation. The ancient philosophical schools understood that conversion was impossible outside regular spiritual exercises practiced within a community. This was the very tradition the apostle Paul is referring to with his repeated metaphors of running (1 Cor. 9:24; Gal. 2:2; 5:7; Phil. 2:16) and spiritual training (1 Tim. 4:8), except we have far greater resources than the Stoics did to win a prize far greater than a mere laurel wreath (1 Cor. 9:25).

We have a Helper—none other than the crucified, resurrected, and ascended Lord—living within us. The Holy Spirit has for us a goal much loftier and grander than self-mastery, which is only a recipe for pride where we succeed and shame where we fail. Rather, our goal is to be conformed to the image of God, that is, for the image of God to be restored and renewed in us. Our goal is to become fully human, just as Christ is fully human.

ONE EXAMPLE: THE EXERCISE OF TALKING BACK

There are plenty of great books out there on spiritual exercises. In closing this chapter, we want to focus on one exercise. This exercise is called the way of "talking back," based on a book by Evagrius of Ponticus entitled *Talking Back*.[26]

In our time, cognitive behavioral therapy (CBT) is a common method that's empirically proven to help patients with distressing emotional and psychological problems. The core of the method is to help patients recognize and correct cognitive distortions—that is, distorted habits of thinking.[27] But the roots of this wisdom can be traced not to modern psychology but to ancient wisdom.

Before anyone had heard of CBT, Evagrius was teaching his students the necessity of learning to talk back to your distressing emotions and thoughts. You are not your thoughts! Evagrius used the method that Christ had utilized in the desert against Satan when he was tempted. He used verses from Scripture to confound the lies being whispered in his ear (Luke 4:1–12).

The exercise is simple. When you find yourself feeling overwhelmed by a distressing emotion or thought, train yourself (it's an *exercise*!) to examine what's underneath that emotion and to reply with a Scripture verse. The sixth-century Saint Benedict put it like this: "As soon as wrongful thoughts come into your heart, dash them against Christ"[28] (which is Benedict's colorful and innovative interpretation of Psalm 137:9).

THE CROSS BEFORE ME

You take those thoughts when they creep up. You recognize them, name them, and then dash them against the rock that is Christ. Evagrius points to the Psalms because it's there that we can see David doing this very thing. When he was distressed, he talked back to himself ("Why, my soul, are you downcast?" [Ps. 42:5 NIV]) and reminded himself of the truth ("God is our refuge and strength" [Ps. 46:1]).

You are not your thoughts or your emotions. It sounds so simple, but it's so profound. The ability to name and untangle yourself from your emotions—not to be hijacked by them but to respond to them—takes discipline. It's not a thought experiment. It takes exercise … in this case, the exercise of talking back.

So you find yourself in bed, tossing and turning, unable to sleep, riddled with anxiety and worry, playing the "what if" game, and absorbed in fretting over things that are outside your control. What can you do? What does the cruciform life ask you to do? The cross is your guide. It tells you to die to your own self-will and your own self-understanding. This worry is a weed. In this case, you could apply the truth of a Scripture verse like this one: "If we live, we live to the Lord, and if we die, we die to the Lord. So then, whether we live or whether we die, we are the Lord's" (Rom. 14:8).

"God, my life is in your sovereign hands, so I leave to your wise disposition whatever you have for me, in life or in death. I am not my own but belong to you, so I do not lean on my understanding but entrust my future to your gracious disposition."

That's talking back—in this instance to the weed of worry. You don't indulge it. "Fret not yourself" (Ps. 37:8).

We should add that Bible memorization is a necessary and powerful exercise to aid in talking back. If we have memorized Scripture, we will have ready responses to talk back to these false thoughts. Even more basically, the things we memorize shape us; they run through our minds and help us reimagine the world—to see it with the eyes of Christ.

Thus, Paul's exhortation "Do not be conformed to this world, but be transformed by the renewing of your mind" (Rom. 12:2) applies not only to our intellects but to our imaginations as well. And this includes the words we speak both to others and to ourselves.

Our words shape the way we see the world. How we think affects how we feel; therefore, how we choose to set our minds will affect our disposition.[29] Resetting your mind is a vital activity of the imagination. By having the true words of Scripture in our minds, we begin to see the world anew. This is an essential part of reimagining the good life.[30]

TRAINING NOT TRYING

It is so important to remember that you are training not trying. As we were working on this chapter, I (Rankin) read that phrase twice in one week. Once, in the *New York Times* in an article about how to be more patient: "Train, don't try. The most common mistake people make is thinking sheer will can turn them into a more patient person, Dr. Schnitker said. If you do that, she cautions, you're setting yourself up to fail. Just as marathon runners don't run a marathon on their first day of hitting the trails, people who are serious about cultivating patience shouldn't expect immediate results. 'You want to train, not try, for patience,' she said. 'It's important to do it habitually.'"[31]

The same idea came up in a book by John Ortberg, *The Life You've Always Wanted: Spiritual Disciplines for Ordinary People.* Ortberg says that the idea of training instead of trying has been the most helpful principle in his understanding of spiritual formation.[32] Both authors agree sheer willpower won't enable us to die to ourselves. It will almost certainly lead us instead to both excessive self-concern and pride over any progress we think we are making because we are trying so hard. That's a recipe for exhaustion, failure, and discouragement.

The key, the psychology professor quoted in the *New York Times* says, is to "connect [the habit] to that bigger picture story of why it's important." She is saying that you need a narrative to guide your training so that your virtue will grow like a muscle.[33] This is what the gospel of Jesus Christ gives us. The beauty of holiness and the joy of communion—become what you are!—give us this bigger narrative to help us make sense of this strange call to the cruciform life. Training needs to be rooted in reimagining, in a new vision of God's reality.

So back to the example above—when you are eaten up with worry, where is the sense of peace going to come from? How can you know in that moment that come what may, whatever happens will be for your good? You can't give peace to yourself. What voice is going to "talk back" and tell you, "Fear not ... When you pass through the waters, I will be with you; and through the rivers, they shall not overwhelm you" (Isa. 43:1–2)?

You can *train* in the exercise of "talking back," reminding your heart of what is true: "He drew me up from the pit of destruction, out of the miry bog, and set my feet upon a rock, making my steps secure" (Ps. 40:2).

While talking back may seem like a solitary affair, you actually can't do this alone. Learning to love and live the cruciform life takes a community, a community of Christ followers committed to Christ's way. More powerful than talking back to yourself is when the voice of a friend speaks the truth of Christ over you, especially in those times when you can't feel it yourself. But remember—in the cruciform life, the real test is not the crisis but the everyday moments:

> We do not need the grace of God to withstand crises—human nature and pride are sufficient for us to face the stress and strain magnificently. But it does require the supernatural grace of God to live twenty-four hours of every day as a saint, going through drudgery, and living an ordinary, unnoticed, and ignored existence as a disciple

of Jesus. It is ingrained in us that we have to do exceptional things for God—but we do not. We have to be exceptional in the ordinary things of life, and holy on the ordinary streets, among ordinary people—and this is not learned in five minutes.[34]

Keeping the cross before us is difficult, but as we have argued in this book, it is the way to the good, true, and beautiful life.

CONCLUSION

And they compelled a passerby, Simon of Cyrene, who was coming in from the country, the father of Alexander and Rufus, to carry his cross.

Mark 15:21

We don't know much about Simon, which is important because it means that Simon could have been pretty much anyone. We are told that he was from Cyrene, which means he was far from home when he encountered Jesus.[1]

If you're tempted to romanticize the scene and think that Simon looked with compassion at the stranger staggering toward him, then you've not realized what crucifixion meant to the ancient Jews, Greeks, and Romans. It was a public humiliation reserved for the worst sort of criminals. Recall that Jesus had already been so severely beaten that he could now barely walk. Blood, sweat, and dirt stained his face and body.

Simon did not volunteer to help. He was "compelled," presumably because Jesus had become so weak the soldiers were afraid he would collapse before he got to the place of his crucifixion. Like taking off a heavy jacket, he would have dropped the beam at Simon's feet. This was most likely the first time Simon had seen Jesus. Simon stooped down and took up the cross, and Luke tells us, followed behind him.

The scene reminds us of Jesus' words, "If anyone would come after me, let him deny himself and take up his cross and follow me" (Matt. 16:24). But what's surprising is that Simon had not been following Jesus before now. Luke tells us he was "coming in from the country" (23:26) when he was seized and compelled to take up the cross and follow behind.

Simon's life changed that day. Beneath the cross of Jesus.

This book has been about that day coming for you, dear reader. You were going about your business when whatever plans you had for your life were interrupted. You were seized. Something happened to knock you off whatever mountain you had been climbing. Some failure. Some diagnosis. Some phone call. Some revelation. Some pain. Transformation usually has to do with pain.

For a while, it can feel like a heavy burden has been placed upon your shoulders. Like Simon, you may feel a long way from home. Of course, Simon did not have a choice. But you do. How will you respond?

We are never told precisely why Simon had to carry the cross. Jesus had been severely flogged, so maybe he was unable to keep carrying the burden, but we are never told that. The writer Craig

Barnes conjectures that perhaps the reason Simon had to carry Jesus' cross had less to do with Jesus' condition than it had to do with Simon's. Perhaps, Barnes says, it was a tremendous grace in Simon's life.

Maybe because of that cross, he looked up and saw a whole new vision of Jesus. Maybe that day marked a turning point in his life. Maybe he found courage in that moment because he saw that Jesus went before him and he realized he was sharing in his sufferings. Maybe he realized that even though he had to carry it up the hill, Jesus would be the one to die upon it. And he did.

You too may have to carry that cross, maybe for a long time. But since the cross belongs to him, you can know that in the end it will lead to more life than you've ever known.

You didn't want this. But it is time beneath that cross that can bring deep change to your life.

Why do people often say, "I wouldn't trade any of this for the grace I've received in having gone through this"? Not because suffering is good, but only because it was beneath that cross that they finally came to understand that no one who carries the cross of Jesus is the same person he or she was before it was laid upon his or her shoulders.

The cross is where things get crucified; it's where the old life dies. In calling us to deny ourselves, Jesus is not talking about giving up chocolate. He's talking about giving up whatever you thought you needed to hold yourself up, to justify your life, all these years until you were seized by a strange affection. And that giving up is always painful. Wrenching. It feels like death.

But, just like Simon, you may look up from that cross and realize that Jesus is leading you home. Not to Cyrene, but to a home you've never been to before. Everything Jesus calls you toward, he endured first and for you. Simon climbed a hill, but Jesus went to hell.

We've argued in this book that the cross is not only the instrument of our salvation. It is that instrument. But it's also a new interpretive lens for all reality.

We've taken some of the big words that are important to our lives and our moments—*freedom, work, love, suffering, joy*—and shown how they can be, how they must be, reinterpreted in light of the cross. We could have added more chapters and we hope that you, our readers, will in your imaginations.

"Cruciform Power"

"Cruciform Friendship"

"Cruciform Hospitality"

"Cruciform Justice"

"Cruciform Mission"

"Cruciform Education"

"Cruciform Leadership"

"Cruciform _____"

That's the point: "Cruciform _____." Everything important to you, every value and aspiration, every habit, every fear, must now be reinterpreted in light of the cross.

We began this book with Aristotle, Pascal, Thomas Merton, and Anne Frank, all agreeing that all people seek happiness but noting the tragedy that we don't know what will lead to the good and beautiful life we are frantically searching for.

As Merton writes, "Why do we spend our lives striving to be something that we would never want to be, if only we knew what we wanted? Why do we waste our time doing things which, if we only stopped to think about them, are just the opposite of what we were made for?"[2]

But we've seen in this book that Jesus shows us who we were made to be and redeemed to become: humble, holy, happy, kind, patient, and compassionate. Of course this is the good and beautiful life! We must expect more.

This has not been a self-help book. Jesus died to enable us to live a fully human life, and his Spirit within us now enables us to pursue what his love obligates we do—walk in a manner worthy of the gospel.

Our culture is having a wisdom contest about how to live a fully human life. And each of us is participating by virtue of the choices we make and the desires we pursue.

The cruciform life is God's way, God's wisdom, for the good and beautiful life he intends for the creatures he loves.

We can't say for sure, but Mark introduces Simon by telling us the names of his sons, Alexander and Rufus, as if the church would recognize their names, which would only be true if they had become a part of the church, which suggests that their dad had become a disciple of Jesus.

May you, like Simon, be seized beneath the cross of Jesus and find a new life.

ACKNOWLEDGMENTS

FROM RANKIN WILBOURNE

The seed of this book began many years ago when reading Gerhard Forde's *On Being a Theologian of the Cross* and being bowled over by Luther's contrast between the theologian of glory and the theologian of the cross—and realizing I was not a theologian of the cross. My imagination was stirred. The path for me had already been laid by the words of Robert Frost, Blaise Pascal, Fyodor Dostoyevsky, and Bruce Springsteen—all contrarians, who had prepared me for this subversive journey, which I'm still on. Over the course of writing this book, I've often remarked, "Well, I am writing a book on the cruciform life." Truly, unless a grain of wheat falls into the earth and dies ... So, even to the pain of being broken open, for all that has been: thank you. Your scars become the gift you have to give to others.

As with *Union with Christ*, my hope is that this book will find an audience among those who don't normally read books on theology, as it was written to make the theology of the cross accessible to the lives of so-called ordinary men and women, understanding that there are no ordinary people.

I wish to thank, first, my coauthor, Brian, of whom it can be said that he lives the message even better than he writes it. He has been a sermon in shoes of cruciform friendship to me over these many months, as has his remarkable wife, Meg, who always prays and never loses hope. Thank you to Russ for calling me every day. Thank you to Thom for teaching me that tears are tenderness and that he who began a good work ... will! Thank you to Hannah, who helped us with all the notes and understands this book better than the authors. Thank you to Keanu for all your help in research. Thank you to Caroline, who makes time for me from the ends of the earth and for Ben P., who prays for me. Thanks to my spiritual friends: Ben, Chris, Peter, Russ, Stephen P., Hunter, DK, Coach Dallas, John G., Chown, Cagle, and O'Mara. Thanks to Stephen, my agent and friend, and the good people of David C Cook. Thanks to Jack, Emi Bea, and Will, who remind me that healthy people laugh and play, a lot. For Glen and Carole, still learning after all these years.

And to my best friend, the bravest person I know, cheerful in all weathers, who laughs with me every day, who always reminds me on long and dark and silent Saturdays that Sunday is there and that the sun will shine on the far side of the cross. I marvel at you, Morgen. Where did such poise, resolve, *and* kindness meet? Every day is Easter with you beside me.

FROM BRIAN GREGOR

I didn't intend for the cross to become such a central theme in my thinking and writing. I have often started out working on other topics, and they just seem to lead me back to the cross: cruciform philosophy, the cruciform self, and the cruciform life. What amazes me is how the cross calls us to think differently about the big questions. I hope this book helps you do that.

I am thankful to many people for their contributions to this book.

To my coauthor Rankin. I am blessed to have you as my pastor and honored to call you my friend. To be a pastor is to live under a scrutiny like no other: your life, and the lives of your family, are uniquely visible. Thank you, Rankin and Morgen, for modeling the way of the cross.

To Meg, my wife. This book owes so much to you. Your enthusiasm for the project kept me moving when I was discouraged. Your judicious comments helped me sort the good from the bad. And your love reminds me of what this book is about in the first place.

To my son and daughter, Thomas and Esmé. You're great.

To Ben Patterson for your friendship and comments on the manuscript.

To my brother Chris for asking every night whether I worked on the book that day.

To my friends for conversations that helped shape this book: Jared and Jenai; Eames and Toddy; James; Alex Chung; Andrew, Steve, and Evan from my Life on Life group; the South Bay Men's Community Group; my barber Jason; and my friend across the hall, Raul, for hours of dialogue and debate.

NOTES

INTRODUCTION

1. David Shimer, "Yale's Most Popular Class Ever: Happiness," *New York Times*, January 26, 2018, www.nytimes.com/2018/01/26/nyregion/at-yale-class -on-happiness-draws-huge-crowd-laurie-santos.html; "Tal Ben-Shahar," Harvard University, accessed April 11, 2019, https://ethics.harvard.edu /people/tal-ben-shahar.

2. Andre Agassi, *Open: An Autobiography* (New York: Knopf, 2009), 3.

3. Agassi, *Open*, 167.

4. Tom Brady, interview by Steve Kroft, *60 Minutes*, CBS, November 6, 2005, www.cbsnews.com/news/tom-brady-the-winner/3.

5. Thomas Merton, *No Man Is an Island* (Boston: Shambhala, 2005), 132.

6. Blaise Pascal, *Pensées* (New York: E. P. Dutton, 1958), 113.

7. Here's a list (not exhaustive) of books we've read in these categories: bestsellers—*The Happiness Project* by Gretchen Rubin, *Happier* by Tal Ben-Shahar, *The Happiness Equation* by Neil Pasricha; business—*The Happiness Advantage* by Shawn Achor, *The Power of Positive Thinking* by Norman Vincent Peale; scholarly—*The Happiness Hypothesis* by Jonathan Haidt, *Stumbling on Happiness* by Daniel Gilbert; Christian—*The Sermon on the Mount and Human Flourishing* by Jonathan T. Pennington, *Flourishing* by Miroslav Volf, *God and the Art of Happiness* by Ellen T. Charry, *The Bible and the Pursuit of Happiness* by Brent A. Strawn, *The Good and Beautiful*

Life by James Bryan Smith, *Happiness* by Randy Alcorn. All this exuberant positivity has even sparked a backlash, a whole cottage industry rebelling against this wave of sunny optimism, with titles like *Against Happiness: In Praise of Melancholy* by Eric G. Wilson, *Perpetual Euphoria: On the Duty to Be Happy* by Pascal Bruckner and Steven Rendall, *The Wellness Syndrome* by Carl Sederström and André Spicer, and our favorite of the bunch, *Bright-Sided: How Positive Thinking Is Undermining America* by Barbara Ehrenreich.

8. It's not just books, popular and scholarly, that have caught the happiness fever. One author, noting that what makes us happy is largely out of our control, says that we can at least aim to be 10 percent happier. He draws on the emerging science of meditation, and even the fact that "the emerging science of meditation" exists shows us the ascendancy of happiness in the realms of science and psychology. Dan Harris, *10% Happier: How I Tamed the Voice in My Head, Reduced Stress without Losing My Edge, and Found Self-Help That Actually Works—a True Story* (New York: Dey Street Books, 2014). Dr. Martin Seligman introduced positive psychology into the mainstream when he became president of the American Psychological Association in 1998. Since then, his work (most notably *Authentic Happiness*) and many other books and podcasts on the benefits and promises of positive psychology have emerged. Positive psychology is the study of human flourishing and what science has to teach us about what makes for a healthier and happier life. Indeed, the title of one of Dr. Seligman's later bestselling books is *Flourish: A Visionary New Understanding of Happiness and Well-Being*.

9. Laura Hillenbrand, *Unbroken: A World War II Story of Survival, Resilience, and Redemption* (New York: Random House, 2010).

10. One of the elder statesmen of Protestant evangelicalism over the last fifty years, Dr. J. I. Packer, notes that historically communion with God has been understood to be God's highest purpose, the great end to which all creation and God's redemption in Christ are but the means. Communion, he writes, "is the goal to which both theology and preaching must ever point; it is the essence of true religion; it is, indeed, the definition of Christianity." Yet Packer goes on to note that a theme rarely talked about today, much less celebrated, is communion with God made possible through our union with Christ. J. I. Packer, *A Quest for Godliness: A Puritan Vision of the Christian Life* (Wheaton, IL: Crossway, 1990), 202,

215–16. It's the tragic disappearance of this rich biblical theme and some of the debilitating practical consequences of its loss that were the occasion of Rankin's first book, *Union with Christ*. This book is, in many ways, a sequel. If happiness is our communion with God made possible through our union with Christ, how will this communion be experienced? For the importance of seeking God's face in the Christian tradition, see Hans Boersma, *Seeing God: The Beatific Vision in Christian Tradition* (Grand Rapids, MI: Eerdmans, 2018).

11. A point Richard B. Hays makes forcefully and eloquently in his commentary on 1 Corinthians: "The fundamental theological point is that if the cross itself is God's saving event, all human standards of evaluation are overturned." He also writes, "*The word of the cross creates a countercultural world for those who are called.* Because God has confounded the wisdom of this world and shown it to be foolish, Christians must see the world differently and live in light of the wisdom of God. (This should not be confused with Thoreau's 'marching to the beat of a different drummer,' which implies merely individualistic and idiosyncratic behavior.) When people tell us that we must be 'responsible' or 'realistic,' or act in ways that will be 'effective,' we should be wary and ask whose wisdom, whose rationality is being urged upon us. Is it God's?" *First Corinthians* (Louisville, KY: Westminster John Knox, 2011), 30, 38. For a more extensive development of this theme from Hays, see *The Moral Vision of the New Testament: A Contemporary Introduction to New Testament Ethics* (New York: HarperCollins, 1996).

12. The book was Gerhard Forde, *On Being a Theologian of the Cross: Reflections on Luther's Heidelberg Disputation, 1518* (Grand Rapids, MI: Eerdmans, 1997). For Luther the cross is not only the means of our salvation but also a revelation of God. See also Henri Nouwen, *The Selfless Way of Christ: Downward Mobility and the Spiritual Life* (Maryknoll, NY: Orbis Books, 2007); and more recently J. I. Packer, *Weakness Is the Way: Life with Christ Our Strength* (Wheaton, IL: Crossway, 2013); and Jamin Goggin and Kyle Strobel, *The Way of the Dragon or the Way of the Lamb: Searching for Jesus' Path of Power in a Church That Has Abandoned It* (Nashville: Nelson Books, 2017).

13. Martin Luther, *Luther's Commentary on the First Twenty-Two Psalms*, trans. Henry Cole, trans. and ed. John Nikolas Lenker (Sunbury, PA: Lutherans in All Lands, 1903), 289. This was quoted by Forde, who goes on to point

out that in Luther's theology of the cross, *cross* is shorthand for the entire narrative of the crucified and resurrected Jesus. *On Being a Theologian*, 8–9. See also Joshua D. Chatraw and Mark D. Allen, *Apologetics at the Cross: An Introduction for Christian Witness* (Grand Rapids, MI: Zondervan, 2018), which argues the entire apologetic enterprise should start from and be shaped by "the word of the cross."

14. See Charles Cousar's book *A Theology of the Cross: The Death of Jesus in the Pauline Letters* (Minneapolis: Augsburg Fortress, 1990); and Ernst Käsemann's essay "The Saving Significance of the Death of Jesus in Paul," in *Perspectives on Paul* (Philadelphia: Fortress, 1971), 32–59. Also, consult the work of Michael Gorman, especially his book *Cruciformity: Paul's Narrative Spirituality of the Cross* (Grand Rapids, MI: Eerdmans, 2001). Gorman takes Philippians 2:6–11 as Paul's master story, and while we may differ with him on what Paul means by *justification*, Gorman is an important New Testament scholarly voice on the centrality of the theology of the cross for Paul.

15. Similar to his first book, *Union with Christ*, Rankin wanted to take a central biblical theme that was difficult and abstract and make it accessible to a broader audience. It's not a surprise that there aren't a lot of books out there for laypeople on the theology of the cross. It's hard to explain, and once you try, it's even harder to see how this is good news. Beside Forde's book, if you want to read more deeply on the theology of the cross, here are some of the most important titles from the last fifty years: Alister E. McGrath, *Luther's Theology of the Cross: Martin Luther's Theological Breakthrough* (Oxford: Blackwell, 1990); Douglas John Hall, *The Cross in Our Context: Jesus and the Suffering World* (Minneapolis: Augsburg Fortress, 2003); Eberhard Jüngel, *God as the Mystery of the World: On the Foundation of the Theology of the Crucified One in the Dispute between Theism and Atheism*, trans. Darrell L. Guder (Grand Rapids, MI: Wipf and Stock, 2009); Jürgen Moltmann, *The Crucified God* (Minneapolis: Fortress, 2015); Graham Tomlin, *The Power of the Cross: Theology and the Death of Christ in Paul, Luther and Pascal* (Eugene, OR: Wipf and Stock, 2006); Walther von Loewenich, *Luther's Theology of the Cross*, trans. Herbert J. A. Bouman (Minneapolis: Augsburg, 1976); Jeremy R. Treat, *The Crucified King: Atonement and Kingdom in Biblical and Systematic Theology* (Grand Rapids, MI: Zondervan, 2014). Also see Richard B. Gaffin Jr.'s wonderful essay "The Usefulness of the Cross," *Westminster Theological Journal* 41, no. 2 (Spring 1979): 228–46.

16. The line is from Jeremiah Burroughs, *The Rare Jewel of Christian Contentment* (Carlisle, PA: Banner of Truth Trust, reprint 2009), 45.

17. Brian Gregor, *A Philosophical Anthropology of the Cross: The Cruciform Self* (Bloomington, IN: Indiana University Press, 2013).

CHAPTER 1

1. For the definitive treatment of crucifixion in the ancient world, see Martin Hengel, *Crucifixion* (Philadelphia: Fortress, 1977).

2. With respect to Rod Dreher (*How Dante Can Save Your Life* [New York: Regan Arts, 2015]) for the title of this section. You can find a version of this summary of Boethius's life in H. R. James, Poem to Boethius, *The Consolation of Philosophy of Boethius*, trans. H. R. James (London: Elliot Stock, 1897), ix–xi.

3. Boethius, *The Consolation of Philosophy*, trans. and ed. P. G. Walsh (New York: Oxford University Press, 2000), 27, 60–61.

4. Boethius, *The Consolation of Philosophy*, trans. David R. Slavitt (Cambridge, MA: Harvard University Press, 2008), 85–86.

5. Boethius, *The Consolation of Philosophy*, trans. David R. Slavitt, 58.

6. J. I. Packer, *A Quest for Godliness: A Puritan Vision of the Christian Life* (Wheaton, IL: Crossway, 1990), 202.

7. Martin Luther calls this assumed path "the way of glory." The way of glory assumes that we can make our way to God by purifying our minds and becoming virtuous in order to be worthy of entering God's presence.

8. This passage provides the title and epigraph for Charles Marsh's book *Strange Glory: A Life of Dietrich Bonhoeffer* (New York: Knopf, 2014).

9. Richard Bauckham, *Gospel of Glory: Major Themes in Johannine Theology* (Grand Rapids, MI: Baker Academic, 2015), 73. See also Bauckham, *God Crucified: Monotheism and Christology in the New Testament* (Grand Rapids, MI: Eerdmans, 1998). The classic states of Christ's humiliation and exaltation can add to this confusion and suggest that his crucifixion was only a part of his humiliation while his resurrection was his exaltation.

10. Dave Harvey, *Rescuing Ambition* (Wheaton, IL: Crossway, 2010), 25.

11. Anthony C. Thiselton, *The First Epistle to the Corinthians*, The New International Greek Testament Commentary, eds. I. Howard Marshall and Donald A. Hagner (Grand Rapids, MI: Eerdmans, 2000), 1–3, 8, 10–17.

12. David Shimer, "Yale's Most Popular Class Ever: Happiness," *New York Times*, January 26, 2018, www.nytimes.com/2018/01/26/nyregion/at-yale -class-on-happiness-draws-huge-crowd-laurie-santos.html.

13. See Kate Bowler's prophetic *Blessed: A History of the American Prosperity Gospel* (New York: Oxford University Press, 2013) about the rising popularity and marks of prosperity preaching. What's most challenging about her thoroughly researched book is that you leave it convinced that American evangelicalism is different not in kind but only in degree from the prosperity preaching from which it often tries to distinguish itself. In many ways, prosperity preachers are being more honest about their underlying values and convictions.

14. Anthony A. Hoekema, *Created in God's Image* (Grand Rapids, MI: Eerdmans, 1994), 22.

15. Karl Barth, *Church Dogmatics*, ed. G. W. Bromiley and T. F. Torrance, vol. 1, *The Doctrine of the Word of God*, 8–12, *The Revelation of God: The Triune God* (London: T&T Clark, 2010), 91.

16. Blaise Pascal, *Pensées* (New York: E. P. Dutton, 1958), 147.

17. John Calvin, *Institutes of the Christian Religion*, trans. Henry Beveridge (Peabody, MA: Hendrickson, 2009), 458.

18. Thérèse, *Story of a Soul: The Autobiography of Saint Thérèse of Lisieux*, ed. Marc Foley, trans. John Clarke (Washington, DC: ICS Publications, 2005), 422.

19. We were created for communion: communion with God and communion with others. This is a truth we find throughout the Christian tradition, from the biblical texts to thinkers as diverse as Gregory of Nyssa, Thomas Aquinas, Dante, John Paul II, and John Owen, and, more recently, John Zizioulas. The good news of the Christian story is that we are *in* Christ unconditionally. By uniting himself to us, he has made us right with God—justified, sanctified, and redeemed—so we can stand in God's presence. This union with Christ is fixed—a settled matter, a finished reality. John Owen teaches that if union with Christ is a fixed reality, then communion with God is the *way* to genuine human flourishing. See *Communion with the Triune God*, eds. Kelly M. Kapic and Justin Taylor

(Wheaton, IL: Crossway, 2007). This communion comes about by way of the cross: those who seek their own selves will lose them, but those who lose their selves for Christ's sake will find them. The cross is the way to deeper communion with God, therefore deeper flourishing, because this is who God is: the God of the cross.

20. Boethius, *The Consolation of Philosophy*, trans. David R. Slavitt, 58.

21. C. S. Lewis, *The Lion, the Witch and the Wardrobe* (London: HarperCollins, 2015), 142.

22. Suffering was necessary for Paul ("That was to make us rely not on ourselves but on God" [2 Cor. 1:9]); it was necessary for the psalmist ("It is good for me that I was afflicted, that I might learn your statutes" [Ps. 119:71]); and it was necessary even for Jesus himself, perfect though he was. Even he, the Bible dares to say, "learned obedience through what he suffered" (Heb. 5:8).

23. W. H. Auden, "Purely Subjective," in *The Complete Works of W. H. Auden*, ed. Edward Mendelson, vol. 2, *Prose: 1939–1948* (Princeton, NJ: Princeton University Press, 2002), 196–97.

24. Søren Kierkegaard, *The Sickness unto Death: A Christian Psychological Exposition for Upbuilding and Awakening*, trans. and eds. Howard V. Hong and Edna H. Hong (Princeton, NJ: Princeton University Press, 1983), 83.

25. Irenaeus, *Catechism of the Catholic Church* (New York: Doubleday, 1995), 86. We used the common translation of Irenaeus's phrase, although a more literal translation of the Latin *Gloria enim Dei vivens homo* might be "the glory of God is a living man." Irenaeus, *Libros Quinque Adversus Haeresus*, ed. W. Wigan Harvey (Cambridge: Typis Academicis, 1857), 2:219, www .touchstonemag.com/archives/article.php?id=25-05-003-e.

26. Thomas Aquinas, *Summa Theologica: Volume 1, Part 1*, trans. Fathers of the English Dominican Province (New York: Cosimo Classics, 2007), 12. I first heard the phrase "wisdom contest" in an unrecorded talk given by Tim Keller.

27. Sonja Lyubomirsky, *The How of Happiness: A Scientific Approach to Getting the Life You Want* (New York: Penguin, 2007), 14.

CHAPTER 2

1. René Descartes, *Discourse on the Method for Conducting One's Reason Well and for Seeking Truth in the Sciences*, trans. Donald A. Cress, 3rd ed. (Indianapolis: Hackett, 1998), 35.

2. See Ryan Holiday, *The Obstacle Is the Way: The Timeless Art of Turning Trials into Triumph* (New York: Portfolio, 2014); Ryan Holiday, *Ego Is the Enemy: The Fight to Master Our Greatest Opponent* (London: Profile Books, 2017); and Ryan Holiday and Stephen Hanselman, *The Daily Stoic: 366 Meditations on Wisdom, Perseverance, and the Art of Living* (London: Profile Books, 2016). For an overview of this trend, see Jules Evans, *Philosophy for Life and Other Dangerous Situations: Ancient Philosophy for Modern Problems* (Novato, CA: New World Library, 2012).

3. Pierre Hadot, *Philosophy as a Way of Life*, ed. Arnold I. Davidson, trans. Michael Chase (Oxford: Blackwell, 1995).

4. "Introducing the 2018 Spartan Race Heat Category Types," Spartan, accessed April 13, 2019, www.spartan.com/en/race/learn-more/2018-category -types.

5. Charles Taylor, in writing about expressive individualism as a basic assumption of our time, adds that individuality must be lived out "against surrendering to conformity with a model imposed on us from outside." *A Secular Age* (Cambridge, MA: Belknap Press, 2007), 475.

6. See the sad statistics compiled in David Kinnaman and Gabe Lyons, *UnChristian: What a New Generation Thinks about Christianity … and Why It Matters* (Grand Rapids, MI: Baker, 2007), 46–48.

7. See Kate Bowler, *Blessed: A History of the American Prosperity Gospel* (New York: Oxford University Press, 2013).

8. See Jonathan T. Pennington's provocative *The Sermon on the Mount and Human Flourishing: A Theological Commentary* (Grand Rapids, MI: Baker Academic, 2017), which makes a similar argument to ours here. In the Beatitudes Jesus really was laying out a program for the blessed life. For a more popular treatment, see James Bryan Smith, *The Good and Beautiful Life: Putting on the Character of Christ* (Downers Grove, IL: InterVarsity Press, 2009).

9. Josef Pieper, *Happiness and Contemplation*, trans. Richard Winston and Clara Winston (South Bend, IN: St. Augustine's, 1998), 15.

10. David Bentley Hart, *The New Testament: A Translation* (New Haven, CT: Yale University Press, 2017), 7.

11. Friedrich Nietzsche, *Beyond Good and Evil: Prelude to a Philosophy of the Future*, trans. and ed. Walter Kaufmann (New York: Vintage Books, 1989), 60.

12. The Augustine scholar Charles Mathewes observes that the Greeks and Romans expected their gods to be static and unresponsive to humans, and they did not expect any compassion from the gods. If there were to be union with the divine, "the higher never condescends to stoop to the lower; it is rather up to the lower to convert and rise to the higher, and then become assimilated into the same immobile character as the higher principle." *Books That Matter: The City of God* (Chantilly, VA: Great Courses, 2016), 234.

13. C. S. Lewis makes a similar point in *Miracles: A Preliminary Study* (New York: HarperCollins, 2001), 173–213; as does Luc Ferry in *A Brief History of Thought: A Philosophical Guide to Living*, trans. Theo Cuffe (New York: HarperCollins, 2011). Ferry notes that what was so distinct about the Christian message was the notion that the gods actually cared about the lives of individual human beings and even loved human beings.

14. Plato, *The Republic*, trans. and ed. Allan Bloom (New York: Basic Books, 2016), 381c.

15. Charles Norris Cochrane, *Christianity and Classical Culture: A Study of Thought and Action from Augustus to Augustine* (Indianapolis: Liberty Fund, 2003), 28, 127, 174. But also see Werner Jaegar's three-volume masterwork, *Paideia: The Ideals of Greek Culture*, trans. Gilbert Highet (New York: Oxford University Press, 1945), which charts the course of how this quest for the good life turned inward in the wake of the fall of the Greek city-states. When stability in Athens could no longer be counted on to support the good life, the quest turned inward and the link between virtue and happiness was set.

16. For information on crucifixion being reserved for rebels, robbers, violent criminals, and slaves, see Martin Hengel, *Crucifixion in the Ancient World and the Folly of the Cross*, trans. John Bowden (Philadelphia: Fortress, 1977), 46, 51.

17. According to Fleming Rutledge, crucifixion "was a form of advertisement, or public announcement—this person is the scum of the earth, not fit to live, more an insect than a human being. The crucified wretch was pinned up like a specimen. Crosses were not placed out in the open for convenience or sanitation, but for maximum public exposure." *The Crucifixion: Understanding the Death of Jesus Christ* (Grand Rapids, MI: Eerdmans, 2015), 91–92.

18. Russell Moore, "Is Penal Substitutionary Atonement Immoral?" April 14, 2017, *Signposts* podcast, www.russellmoore.com/search/Is+Penal +Substitutionary+Atonement+Immoral/.

19. Rutledge, *Crucifixion*, 92.

20. Alasdair MacIntyre, *After Virtue: A Study in Moral Theory* (London: Bloomsbury Academic, 2013), 215.

21. See Richard B. Hays, *The Conversion of the Imagination: Paul as Interpreter of Israel's Scripture* (Grand Rapids, MI: Eerdmans, 2005). See also Hays, *The Moral Vision of the New Testament: A Contemporary Introduction to New Testament Ethics* (New York: HarperCollins, 1996).

22. Paul distinguishes between two opposite modes of speech or discourse (logos): on the one hand, the word that is clever, eloquent, or wise in a worldly sense; and on the other hand, the word of the cross, which is foolishness to the world (1 Cor. 1:17–21). Paul writes that Christ had sent him to proclaim the gospel, "not in cleverness of speech, so that the cross of Christ would not be made void" (v. 17 NASB). This is an important point. In the ancient world, speech or logos was a means to power, wealth, and influence. Anyone who wanted to succeed in public life had to be able to speak persuasively. There was therefore a strong market for sophists and rhetoricians, who taught the art of persuasive speech and disputation. If you were going to speak in public, you had to be ready to speak to win. That context casts Paul's words about how he spoke (2:1–5) and what he spoke (1:18–21) in an important light.

23. B. A. Gerrish, *Grace and Reason: A Study in the Theology of Luther* (Eugene, OR: Wipf and Stock, 2005), 103.

24. For example, Plato argues that the Greek poets told false stories about the gods, describing them as vicious, petty beings at war with one another and interfering arbitrarily in human affairs (*Republic* 378b–d, 380a–b). Instead, Plato shifts toward a kind of rational monotheism, arguing that "the god

must surely always be described such as he is" (379a). The true essence of the god is to be just, good, simple (rather than composite), unchanging, and unaltered by outside forces (379b–381a).

25. It's worth reflecting on how even "good theology" about God can become a theology of glory when it's used to keep the real God at a distance and his demands an abstraction. Theology becomes a defense mechanism: thinking about God—thinking good and proper thoughts about God—becomes an excuse not to submit, repent, and follow the living God.

26. Bob Smietana, "Most Churchgoers Say God Wants Them to Prosper Financially," LifeWay Research, July 31, 2013, https://lifewayresearch .com/2018/07/31/most-churchgoers-say-god-wants-them-to-prosper -financially.

27. Mark Galli, "God's Peace Is Not Always God's," *Christianity Today*, April 20, 2018, www.christianitytoday.com/ct/2018/may/gods-peace-is-not-always -gods.html.

28. Ross Douthat sums up this logic well: "If you fail to master everyday events, and fall into struggles and suffering, it's a sign that you just haven't prayed hard enough, or trusted faithfully enough, or thought big enough, or oth- erwise behaved the way a child of God really should." *Bad Religion: How We Became a Nation of Heretics* (New York: Free Press, 2012), 191.

29. This is a point that Martin Luther makes in theses 19–21 of his *Heidelberg Disputation*, in *Martin Luther's Basic Theological Writings*, ed. Timothy F. Lull (Minneapolis: Fortress, 2005), 57.

30. "Nike Women & the 'Make Yourself' Movement," *NMICT&Dev Group 5* (blog), October 29, 2011, http://wpmu.mah.se/nmict11group5/2011/10 /29/nike-women-the-make-yourself-movement.

31. See the explosion of books on meditation, including Sam Harris, *Waking Up: A Guide to Spirituality without Religion* (New York: Simon & Schuster, 2014); and Dan Harris, *10% Happier: How I Tamed the Voice in My Head, Reduced Stress without Losing My Edge, and Found Self-Help That Actually Works—a True Story* (New York: Dey Street Books, 2014).

32. See chapter 7 of Douthat's *Bad Religion*, entitled "The God Within" (211–41), for an accessible overview of these patterns in American religious—or rather, "spiritual"—life.

33. As Philip Rieff recognizes in his prescient 1966 book, *The Triumph of the Therapeutic: Uses of Faith after Freud* (1966; repr., Wilmington, DE: ISI Books, 2006). For the therapeutic person, there is "nothing at stake beyond a manipulatable sense of well-being" (10). This means ceasing "to seek any salvation other than amplitude in living itself" (16). "Men already feel freer to live their lives with a minimum of pretense to anything more grand than sweetening the time" (17). "Not the good life but better living is the therapeutic standard" (48).

34. John Henry Newman, "Christian Repentance," in *Selected Sermons, Prayers, and Devotions*, eds. John F. Thornton and Susan B. Varenne (New York: Vintage Books, 1999), 123.

CHAPTER 3

1. Ingmar Bergman, introduction to *The Seventh Seal: A Film*, trans. Lars Malmström and David Kushner (New York: Simon & Schuster, 1960), 8–9. Thanks to Webster Younce for this illustration.

2. Brené Brown, "Finding Our Way to True Belonging," Ideas.TED.com, September 11, 2017, https://ideas.ted.com/finding-our-way-to-true -belonging; *Merriam-Webster*, s.v. "paradox," accessed April 15, 2019, www.merriam-webster.com/dictionary/paradox.

3. Carl Jung, quoted in Richard Rohr, *Falling Upward: A Spirituality for the Two Halves of Life* (San Francisco: Jossey-Bass, 2011), 58.

4. Salvador Dalí, *The Secret Life of Salvador Dalí*, trans. Haakon M. Chevalier (New York: Dover, 1993), 1.

5. John R. W. Stott, *The Message of the Sermon on the Mount* (Leicester, UK: InterVarsity, 1978), 160.

6. *Moneyball*, directed by Bennett Miller (Culver City, CA: Columbia Pictures, 2011).

7. The reflections on John 12 are from Dave Harvey's book, *Rescuing Ambition* (Wheaton, IL: Crossway, 2010), 19–21. Harvey also speaks of our ambition being "corrupted" and "converted." Harvey's is one of the few books dedicated exclusively to the important topic of ambition in the Christian life, and his book helped frame how this chapter was laid out. It was in

this book that I heard the Timothy Dwight story and read William Carey's statement.

8. C. S. Lewis, "Answers to Questions on Christianity," in *God in the Dock: Essays on Theology and Ethics,* ed. Walter Hooper (Grand Rapids, MI: Eerdmans, 2014), 45–46.

9. Harvey, *Rescuing Ambition*, 41.

10. Timothy Dwight, "Sermon XXVII: On the Love of Distinction," in *Sermons*, vol. 1 (New Haven, CT: Hezekiah Howe and Durrie & Peck, 1828), 503, 508, 512.

11. "Exploring these issues will bring us to the difficult awareness that our ministries must be displaced by the ministry of Jesus. Displacement is more than relinquishment. Displacement is not an invitation to let Jesus take over by letting him in on our territory. Rather, we must be bumped aside firmly, perhaps mortifyingly. Otherwise we will never let go of our grip on our ministries. We are too attached to them and to their payoff, even if at times the payoff is negative. Displacement literally means the death of our ministries.… The crucifixion of ministry by the process of painful displacement by the ministry of Jesus is staggering good news for ministers and for the people among whom we minister." Andrew Purves, *The Crucifixion of Ministry: Surrendering Our Ambitions to the Service of Christ* (Downers Grove, IL: InterVarsity Press, 2007), 13–14.

12. Purves, *Crucifixion of Ministry*, 24.

13. There's a wonderful children's book that depicts this: Trina Paulus, *Hope for the Flowers* (Mahwah, NJ: Paulist, 1972). For a recent exploration, see David Brooks, *The Second Mountain: The Quest for a Moral Life* (New York: Random House, 2019).

14. Purves, *Crucifixion of Ministry*, 25–26.

15. Jamin Goggin and Kyle Strobel, *The Way of the Dragon or the Way of the Lamb: Searching for Jesus' Path of Power in a Church That Has Abandoned It* (Nashville: Nelson Books, 2017), 127.

16. J. I. Packer, quoted in Goggin and Strobel, *Way of the Dragon*, 23. See also J. I. Packer, *Weakness Is the Way: Life with Christ Our Strength* (Wheaton, IL: Crossway, 2013).

17. *The Natural*, directed by Barry Levinson (Culver City, CA: TriStar Pictures, 1984).

18. Bernard Malamud, *The Natural* (New York: Farrar, Straus and Giroux, 2003), 152.

19. J. R. R. Tolkien, "On Fairy-Stories," in *Tree and Leaf* (London: HarperCollins, 2001), 54.

20. As Dorothy L. Sayers wrote, "The worker's first duty is to *serve the work*." "Why Work?," in *Letters to a Diminished Church: Passionate Arguments for the Relevance of Christian Doctrine* (Nashville: W Publishing, 2004), 135.

21. C. S. Lewis, *The Screwtape Letters* (New York: HarperCollins, 2001), 71.

22. Likewise, God "wants him, in the end, to be so free from any bias in his own favour that he can rejoice in his own talents as frankly and gratefully as in his neighbour's talents—or in a sunrise, an elephant, or a waterfall. He wants each man, in the long run, to be able to recognise all creatures (even himself) as glorious and excellent things. He wants to kill their animal self-love as soon as possible; but it is His long-term policy ... to restore to them a new kind of self-love—a charity and gratitude for all selves, including their own; when they have really learned to love their neighbours as themselves, they will be allowed to love themselves as their neighbours." Lewis, *Screwtape Letters*, 71–72.

23. François Fénelon, "The Uses of Humiliation," in *The Complete Fénelon*, trans. and eds. Robert J. Edmonson and Hal M. Helms (Brewster, MA: Paraclete, 2008), 95–96.

24. Malamud, *The Natural*, 152.

25. Brooks, *Second Mountain*, xiv.

26. John Stott, *The Message of the Sermon on the Mount* (Downers Grove, IL: InterVarsity Press), 173.

CHAPTER 4

1. Joseph Conrad, *Lord Jim* (Garden City, NY: Doubleday, 1920), 58.

2. Julian, *Revelations of Divine Love*, ed. Grace Warrack (London: Methuen, 1920), 153, paraphrased in Richard Rohr, *Falling Upward: A Spirituality for the Two Halves of Life* (San Francisco: Jossey-Bass, 2011), 58.

3. Bernard, *On the Steps of Humility and Pride*, in *Bernard of Clairvaux: Selected Works*, trans. G. R. Evans (Mahwah, NY: Paulist, 1987), 121.

4. Aristotle, *Nicomachean Ethics*, trans. Robert C. Bartlett and Susan D. Collins (Chicago: University of Chicago Press, 2011), 1123b1–1124b13.

5. Augustine, "Letter CXVIII," in *The Works of Aurelius Augustine, Bishop of Hippo*, ed. Marcus Dods, vol. 13, *Letters of Saint Augustine, Bishop of Hippo*, trans. J. G. Cunningham, vol. 2 (Edinburgh: T. & T. Clark, 1875), 109.

6. Andrew Murray, *Humility* (New Kensington, PA: Whitaker House, 1982), 16.

7. Dietrich von Hildebrand, *Humility: Wellspring of Virtue* (Manchester, NH: Sophia Institute, 1997), 93.

8. Bernard, *On the Steps of Humility and Pride*, 103.

9. C. S. Lewis, *Mere Christianity* (New York: HarperOne, 2001), 128.

10. "I should call him blessed and holy to whom it is given to experience even for a single instant something which is rare indeed in this life. To lose yourself as though you did not exist and to have no sense of yourself, to be emptied out of yourself (Phil 2:7) and almost annihilated, belongs to heavenly not to human love. And if indeed any mortal is rapt for a moment or is, so to speak, admitted for a moment to this union, at once the world presses itself on him (Gal 1:4), the day's wickedness troubles him, the mortal body weighs him down, bodily needs distract him, he fails because of the weakness of his corruption and—more powerfully than these—brotherly love calls him back. Alas, he is forced to come back to himself, to fall again into his affairs, and to cry out wretchedly, 'Lord, I endure violence; fight back for me" (Is 38:14), and, 'Unhappy man that I am, who will free me from the body of this death?' (Rom 7:24)." Bernard, *On Loving God*, in *Bernard of Clairvaux: Selected Works*, 195. The idea of the ladder of humility is from *The Rule of St. Benedict*, written in the sixth century. Benedict writes, "The sixth step of humility is that we are content with the lowest and most menial treatment, and regard ourselves as a poor and worthless worker in whatever task we are given.... The seventh step of humility is that we not only admit with our tongues but are also convinced in our hearts that we are inferior to all and of less value, humbling ourselves ..." (Joan Chittister, *Rule of Benedict: A Spirituality for the 21st Century*, Spiritual Legacy Series [n.p., The Crossroad Publishing Company, 89–91, Kindle edition]). Benedict's words shock our sensibilities but perhaps remind us of Paul's confession, "I am the chief of sinners" (see 1 Tim. 1:15 KJV). See *The Rule of St. Benedict in English*, ed. Timothy Fry

(Collegeville, MN: Liturgical, 1982), 32–38. Seeing ourselves as the chief of sinners is not self-hatred but is intended to move us to consider others "more significant than [ourselves]" (Phil. 2:3).

11. Jeremy Taylor, *The Rule and Exercises of Holy Living*, in Richard J. Foster and James Bryan Smith, eds., *Devotional Classics*, rev. ed. (New York: HarperOne, 2005), 244.

12. See Jim Collins, *Good to Great: Why Some Companies Make the Leap … and Others Don't* (New York: HarperCollins, 2001), 12–13.

13. Lewis, *Mere Christianity*, 128.

14. Beth Moore, *Praying God's Word: Breaking Free from Spiritual Strongholds* (Nashville: B&H, 2009), 59–60.

15. Jeremy Taylor, *The Rule and Exercises of Holy Living* (Cambridge, MA: E. P. Dutton, 1876), 125.

16. *Merriam-Webster*, s.v. "humble," accessed April 16, 2019, www.merriam -webster.com/dictionary/humble#etymology.

17. Compare Reinhold Niebuhr's definition of *sin* as "the unwillingness of man to acknowledge his creatureliness and dependence upon God and his effort to make his own life independent and secure." *The Nature and Destiny of Man: A Christian Interpretation*, vol. 1, *Human Nature* (Louisville, KY: Westminster John Knox, 1996), 137–38.

18. Kathleen Norris, *Amazing Grace: A Vocabulary of Faith* (New York: Riverhead Books, 1999), 166–67.

19. Dietrich Bonhoeffer, *The Cost of Discipleship*, trans. R. H. Fuller and Irmgard Booth (New York: Touchstone, 1995), 138–39.

20. Keith Getty, Kristyn Getty, and Graham Kendrick, "My Worth Is Not in What I Own," Getty Music, 2014, www.gettymusic.com/my-worth-is-not -in-what-i-own.

21. Thomas Merton, *The Seven Storey Mountain: An Autobiography of Faith* (Orlando, FL: Harcourt, 1999), 323.

22. Matthew B. Crawford, *The World beyond Your Head: On Becoming an Individual in an Age of Distraction* (New York: Farrar, Straus and Giroux, 2015). See also the work of Hubert Dreyfus and Sean Dorrance Kelly on this point: *All Things Shining: Reading the Western Classics to Find Meaning in a Secular Age* (New York: Free Press, 2011).

23. Von Hildebrand, *Humility*, 68.

24. Von Hildebrand, *Humility*, 63.

CHAPTER 5

1. Karl Barth, *Barth in Conversation*, ed. Eberhard Busch, vol. 1, 1959–1962 (Louisville, KY: Westminster John Knox, 2017), 190–91.

2. Blaise Pascal, *Pensées de Pascal*, ed. Ernest Havet (Paris, 1852), 19.

3. Alexis de Tocqueville, *Democracy in America*, trans. and eds. Harvey C. Mansfield and Delba Winthrop (Chicago: University of Chicago Press, 2002), 464, 484.

4. Ross Douthat, *Bad Religion: How We Became a Nation of Heretics* (New York: Free Press, 2012).

5. *Merriam-Webster*, s.v. "heresy," accessed April 18, 2019, www.merriam -webster.com/dictionary/heresy.

6. Jean-Jacques Rousseau, *On the Social Contract*, ed. David Wootton, trans. Donald A. Cress, 2nd ed. (Indianapolis: Hackett, 2019), 3.

7. John Milton, *Paradise Lost* (London: John Bumpus, 1821), 11.

8. *The Devil's Advocate*, directed by Taylor Hackford (Burbank, CA: Warner Bros., 1997).

9. *Frozen*, directed by Chris Buck and Jennifer Lee (Burbank, CA: Walt Disney Animation Studios, 2013).

10. "I'm Free," by Mick Jagger and Keith Richards, released September 24, 1965, track 12 on *Out of Our Heads*, Decca Records.

11. *The LEGO Movie*, directed by Phil Lord and Christopher Miller (Burbank, CA: Warner Bros., 2014).

12. Planned Parenthood of Southeastern Pa. v. Casey, 505 U.S. 833, 851 (1992).

13. Augustine, *On Free Choice of the Will*, trans. and ed. Thomas Williams (Indianapolis: Hackett, 1993), 11.

14. Augustine, *On Free Choice*, 25.

15. Augustine, *On Free Choice*, 26.

16. Augustine, *Confessions*, trans. Henry Chadwick (New York: Oxford University Press, 2008), 3.

17. Edwin Hall, ed., *The Shorter Catechism of the Westminster Assembly, with Analysis and Scripture Proofs* (Philadelphia: Presbyterian Board of Publication, 1919), 5.

18. George MacDonald, "Kingship," in *Unspoken Sermons Third Series*, Christian Classics Ethereal Library, accessed April 18, 2019, www.ccel.org /ccel/macdonald/unspoken3.vii.html.

19. MacDonald, "Kingship."

20. MacDonald, "Kingship."

21. Excerpt from Christina Rossetti, "Who Shall Deliver Me?," in *The Poetical Works of Christina Georgina Rossetti*, ed. William Michael Rossetti (London: Macmillan, 1904), 238.

22. Blaise Pascal, *Pensées* (New York: E. P. Dutton, 1958), 131.

23. Jean-Paul Sartre, "The Humanism of Existentialism," in *Jean-Paul Sartre: Essays in Existentialism*, ed. Wade Baskin (New York: Citadel, 1988), 36.

24. Considering John Barclay's important observation that gifts in the ancient world always carried reciprocal obligations. John Barclay, *Paul and the Gift* (Grand Rapids, MI: Eerdmans, 2017), 11, 24. For this reason and others, *unconditional* might not be the best modern word to describe God's grace, but the idea of unmerited favor remains.

25. Martin Luther, *On Christian Liberty* (Minneapolis: Fortress, 2003), 2.

26. Søren Kierkegaard, *Works of Love*, trans and eds. Howard V. Hong and Edna H. Hong (Princeton, NJ: Princeton University Press, 1998), 486.

27. Kierkegaard, *Works of Love*, 9–10.

28. Barth, *Barth in Conversation*, 191.

29. Victor Hugo, *Les Misérables*, trans. Charles E. Wilbour (New York: Knopf, 1997), 1.

CHAPTER 6

1. Alain de Botton, "Why You Will Marry the Wrong Person," *New York Times*, May 28, 2016, www.nytimes.com/2016/05/29/opinion/sunday/why-you -will-marry-the-wrong-person.html.2.

2. De Botton, "Why You Will Marry the Wrong Person."

3. Alain de Botton, interview by Krista Tippett, "Alain de Botton—the True Hard Work of Love and Relationships," *On Being*, February 9, 2017, https://onbeing.org/programs/alain-de-botton-the-true-hard-work-of-love -and-relationships-aug2018.

4. De Botton, "Why You Will Marry the Wrong Person."

5. W. H. Auden, "XII," in *Twelve Songs*, in *W. H. Auden: Collected Poems*, ed. Edward Mendelson (New York: Modern Library, 2007), 144.

6. Charles Wesley, "And Can It Be," in John R. Tyson, *Assist Me to Proclaim: The Life and Hymns of Charles Wesley* (Grand Rapids, MI: Eerdmans, 2007), 49.

7. Hans Urs von Balthasar, *Love Alone Is Credible*, trans. D. C. Schindler (San Francisco: Ignatius, 2004), 61, emphasis added.

8. Jonathan Edwards, *Charity and Its Fruits; or, Christian Love as Manifested in the Heart and Life*, ed. Tryon Edwards (London: James Nisbet, 1852), 13.

9. Edwards, *Charity and Its Fruits*, 25.

10. *Merriam-Webster*, s.v. "coup de grâce," accessed April 20, 2019, www .merriam-webster.com/dictionary/coup%20de%20grace.

11. Charles Price Jones, "Deeper, Deeper in the Love of Jesus," Hymnary.org, accessed April 20, 2019, https://hymnary.org/text/deeper_deeper_in_the _love_of_jesus.

12. Lewis B. Smedes, *Love within Limits: A Realist's View of 1 Corinthians 13* (Grand Rapids, MI: Eerdmans, 1978).

13. John Piper, "A Christian Hedonist Looks at 'Love within Limits,'" Desiring God, August 1, 1979, www.desiringgod.org/articles/a-christian-hedonist -looks-at-love-within-limits.

14. B. B. Warfield, *The Emotional Life of Our Lord* (Cambridge: Ravino Books, 2013), n.p.

15. Stephen R. Covey, *The 7 Habits of Highly Effective People: Powerful Lessons in Personal Change* (New York: Simon & Schuster, 2004), 38–39.

16. Adapted from a quotation by Ian Maclaren in *The British Weekly*: "Be pitiful, for every man is fighting a hard battle." "Be Kind; Everyone You Meet Is Fighting a Hard Battle," Quote Investigator, accessed April 20, 2019, https://quoteinvestigator.com/2010/06/29/be-kind.

17. Smedes, *Love within Limits*, 15.

18. See the fine distinction between *kind* and *nice* in Karen Swallow Prior, *On Reading Well: Finding the Good Life through Great Books* (Grand Rapids, MI: Brazos, 2018), 207–8.

19. This encouragement to move toward those who are not being friendly toward you is, of course, not directed to those who are experiencing abuse.

20. De Botton, "Why You Will Marry the Wrong Person."

21. Smedes, *Love Within Limits*, 144.

CHAPTER 7

1. Seneca, *Consolation to Marcia*, in *Hardship and Happiness*, trans. Harry M. Hine (Chicago: University of Chicago Press, 2014), 22.

2. Aristotle, *Nicomachean Ethics*, trans. Robert C. Bartlett and Susan D. Collins (Chicago: University of Chicago Press, 2011), 1099b–1100a.

3. Aristotle, *Nicomachean Ethics*, 1100b–1101a.

4. Epictetus, *The Handbook (The Encheiridion)*, trans. Nicholas P. White (Indianapolis, IN: Hackett, 1983), 12, #3.

5. Diogenes Laertius, *Lives of the Eminent Philosophers*, vol. II, trans. R. D. Hicks (Cambridge, MA: Harvard University Press, 1925, 1931), 549.

6. Laertius, *Lives of the Eminent Philosophers*, 651.

7. Plato, *Phaedo*, trans. David Gallop (Oxford: Oxford University Press, 1993), 78.

8. See Alan E. Lewis, *Between Cross and Resurrection: A Theology of Holy Saturday* (Grand Rapids, MI: Eerdmans, 2001); and Hans Urs von Balthasar's

Mysterium Paschale: The Mystery of Easter, trans. Aidan Nichols, O. P. (San Francisco: Ignatius Press, 1990).

9. Eleanor Stump, *Wandering in Darkness* (Oxford: Oxford University Press, 2010). Here Stump argues persuasively that the difficult questions raised by the problem of suffering are best considered in the context of stories, biblical narratives in particular.

10. Gabriel Marcel, "The Encounter with Evil" in *Tragic Wisdom and Beyond*, trans. Stephen Jolin and Peter McCormick (Evanston, IL: Northwestern University Press, 1973), 140.

11. Marcel, *Tragic Wisdom and Beyond*, 140.

12. Marilyn McCord Adams, "Horrendous Evils and the Goodness of God," *Philosophy of Religion: Selected Readings*, eds. Michael Peterson et al., 4th ed. (Oxford: Oxford University Press, 2010), 333.

13. Chrissie Chapman, *The Night the Angels Came: Miracles of Protection and Provision in Burundi* (Oxford: Monarch Books, 2016), 59–60.

14. For more on this see Douglas John Hall, *The Cross in our Context: Jesus and the Suffering World* (Minneapolis: Fortress, 2003); and the final chapter of Michael J. Gorman's book *Cruciformity*. For the feminist critique of the theology of the cross see Delores S. Williams, *Sisters in the Wilderness*. For a liberation theologian's critique, see Jon Sobrino, *The Principle of Mercy: Taking the Crucified People from the Cross*. In *The Moral Vision of the New Testament*, Richard Hays cites Ellen Charry who "has argued eloquently that the cross and its attendant character-forming implications (humility, self-sacrifice, etc.) are precisely the most powerful theological instruments that can be brought to bear *against* male abuse of power. This seems to [Hays] to be exactly correct." He adds "only that the NT's call for self-sacrificial service cannot be restricted only to men; to exempt women from the summons to be conformed to Christ's example of self-giving would be—paradoxically—to patronize them by excusing them from the call to radical discipleship." Richard Hays, *The Moral Vision of the New Testament: Community, Cross, New Creation* (New York: HarperCollins, 1996), 205.

15. This is a theme of the book of Revelation in particular, see Revelation 12:11. Richard Bauckham in his *The Theology of Revelation* (Cambridge: Cambridge University Press, 1993) argues that Revelation teaches us that this is how God's people conquer and overcome—the way of the lamb who was slain, see in particular pages 73–94. "Jesus Christ won his

comprehensive victory over all evil by suffering witness.... Christians conquer ... by their faithful witness to the truth of God up to and including
death for maintaining this witness. In this way their faithful witness to the
point of death participates in the power of the victory Christ has won by
his faithful witness to the point of death: they conquer 'by the blood of the
lamb' (Rev. 12:11; cf. 7:14)."

16. Friedrich Nietzsche, *On the Genealogy of Morals* in *Basic Writings of
    Nietzsche*, trans. Walter Kaufmann (New York: The Modern Library,
    1968), 472–75.

17. Søren Kierkegaard, *Practice in Christianity*, trans. and eds. Howard V.
    Hong and Edna H. Hong (Princeton, NJ: Princeton University Press,
    1991), 118.

18. Dietrich Bonhoeffer, *Dietrich Bonhoeffer Works*, vol. 4, *Discipleship*,
    eds. Martin Kuske et al., trans. Barbara Green and Reinhard Krauss
    (Minneapolis: Fortress, 2003), 85. It's not just that Jesus was not the
    messiah they were expecting. They didn't want that kind of master because
    they didn't want to be that kind of people—those called to suffer.

19. Christ is our example, but this example is not simply external. We are
    able to follow after him insofar as we are already united to him. "Only
    because he himself already lives his true life in us can we 'walk just as he
    walked' (1 John 2:6), 'act as he acted' (John 13:15), 'love as he loved'
    (Eph. 5:2; John 13:34; 15:12), 'forgive as he forgave' (Col. 3:13), 'have
    the same mind that was in Jesus Christ' (Phil. 2:5), follow the example
    he left for us (1 Peter 2:21), and lose our lives for the sake of our brothers
    and sisters, just as he lost his life for our sake (1 John 3:16)." Bonhoeffer,
    Discipleship, 287.

20. Bonhoeffer, *Discipleship*, 87.

21. Søren Kierkegaard, *Works of Love*, trans. and eds. Howard V. Hong and
    Edna H. Hong (Princeton, NJ: Princeton University Press, 1998), 194.

22. Kierkegaard, *Works of Love*, 195.

23. Kierkegaard, *Works of Love*, 194.

24. Bonhoeffer, *Discipleship*, 85.

25. It's tricky because the church has had an unfortunate legacy of perpetuating
    injustice, promoting and protecting its own interests, often with the cross,
    quite literally, before it. And we should be clear that used as such that is

not the cross of Christ. The cross should never be used to maintain or gather power—to win. And where the church has misused or abused the cross, we should be held to account.

26. Tacitus, *The Annals: The Reigns of Tiberius, Claudius, and Nero*, trans. J. C. Yardley (New York: Oxford University Press, 2008), 15.44.

27. Tacitus, *Annals*, 15.44.

28. A point trenchantly made by Jonathan Haidt in *The Righteous Mind*. Though writing as an atheist, Haidt opens his book by observing that we all tend to be self-righteous in our judgements.

29. Adapted from Tertullian, *The Apology of Tertullian with English Notes and a Preface*, ed. Henry Annesley Woodham, 2nd ed. (Cambridge: J. Deighton, 1850), 170.

30. Søren Kierkegaard, *Kierkegaard's Journals and Notebooks*, vol. 7, *Journals NB15–NB20*, eds. Niels Jørgen Cappelørn et al. (Princeton, NJ: Princeton University Press, 2014), 238.

31. Kierkegaard, *Kierkegaard's Journals and Notebooks*, vol. 5, *Journals NB6–NB10*, eds. Niels Jørgen Cappelørn et al. (Princeton, NJ: Princeton University Press, 2011), 178.

32. Kierkegaard, *Kierkegaard's Journals and Notebooks*, vol. 6, *Journals NB11–NB14*, eds. Niels Jørgen Cappelørn et al. (Princeton, NJ: Princeton University Press, 2012), 187.

33. Elizabeth Rundle Charles, *Chronicles of the Schönberg-Cotta Family by Two of Themselves* (New York: Dodd, Mead, 1868), 321.

34. See Richard Gaffin's essay, "The Usefulness of the Cross." Gaffin writes, "The form of Christ's resurrection power in this world is the fellowship of his sufferings … and so … the essence of Christian existence, as Paul captures it … is: … 'dying, and yet we live; … sorrowful, yet always rejoicing; poor, yet making many rich; having nothing, and yet possessing everything.' (2 Cor. 6:9, 10)" in *Westminster Theological Journal*, vol 41:2 (Spring 1979), 236.

CHAPTER 8

1. No one has said this more persuasively in modern times than John Piper. See *Desiring God: Meditations of a Christian Hedonist*, rev. ed. (Colorado Springs: Multnomah, 2011); or *The Dangerous Duty of Delight: Daring to Make God Your Greatest Desire* (Colorado Springs: Multnomah, 2011), where Piper acknowledges he's picking up the theme from his hero, Jonathan Edwards.

2. Gerard Manley Hopkins, "God's Grandeur," in *Gerard Manley Hopkins: The Major Works*, ed. Catherine Phillips (New York: Oxford University Press, 2009), 128, emphasis added.

3. Friedrich Nietzsche, *The Portable Nietzsche*, trans. and ed. Walter Kaufmann (New York: Penguin, 1982), 453.

4. Nietzsche, quoted in Viktor E. Frankl, *Man's Search for Meaning: An Introduction to Logotherapy*, 4th ed. (Boston: Beacon, 1992), 109.

5. Nietzsche, *The Portable Nietzsche*, 453.

6. Nietzsche, *The Portable Nietzsche*, 454.

7. Friedrich Nietzsche, *The Will to Power*, ed. Walter Kaufmann, trans. Walter Kaufmann and R. J. Hollingdale (New York: Vintage Books, 1968), 543.

8. See Dietrich Bonhoeffer's line "'Seek God, not happiness'—this is the fundamental rule of all meditation. If you seek God alone, you will gain happiness: that is its promise." *Life Together*, trans. John W. Doberstein (New York: Harper & Row, 1954), 84.

9. Taylor writes, "Now the point of bringing out this distinction between human flourishing and goals which go beyond it is this. I would like to claim that the coming of modern secularity in my sense has been coterminous with the rise of a society in which for the first time in history a purely self-sufficient humanism came to be a widely available option. I mean by this a humanism accepting no final goals beyond human flourishing, nor any allegiance to anything else beyond this flourishing. Of no previous society was this true." Charles Taylor, *A Secular Age* (Cambridge, MA: Belknap, 2007), 18, see also 16–20.

10. "You can't pursue the good life without pursuing life. But an existence dedicated to this latter goal alone is not a fully human one." Charles Taylor,

Sources of the Self: The Making of the Modern Identity (Cambridge, MA: Harvard University Press, 1989), 211.

11. Taylor, *Sources of the Self*, 211–12.

12. Taylor, *Sources of the Self*, 213.

13. Taylor, *Sources of the Self*, 211–18. Matthew Myer Boulton makes a similar point in *Life in God: John Calvin, Practical Formation, and the Future of Protestant Theology* (Grand Rapids, MI: Eerdmans, 2011).

14. Dorothy L. Sayers, "Why Work?," in *Letters to a Diminished Church: Passionate Arguments for the Relevance of Christian Doctrine* (Nashville: W Publishing, 2004), 132–33, 135. "The Church's approach to an intelligent carpenter is usually confined to exhorting him not to be drunk and disorderly in his leisure hours, and to come to church on Sundays. What the Church *should* be telling him is this: that the very first demand that his religion makes upon him is that he should make good tables. Church by all means, and decent forms of entertainment, certainly—but what use is all that if in the very center of his life and occupation he is insulting God with bad carpentry? No crooked table legs or ill-fitting drawers ever, I dare swear, came out of the carpenter's shop at Nazareth. Nor, if they did, could anyone believe that they were made by the same hand that made Heaven and earth." "Why Work?," 132.

15. In insisting that work is about more than morality and evangelism, sometimes we forget that being salt and light at work includes, on occasion, talking about Jesus with our coworkers.

16. Charles Taylor, *Secular Age*, 54–59.

17. See Josef Pieper, *Leisure: The Basis of Culture* (San Francisco: Ignatius, 2009).

18. Augustine, *The City of God* 15.22, quoted in Peter Brown, *Augustine of Hippo: A Biography* (Berkeley, CA: University of California, 2000), 325.

19. Augustine, *Homilies on the First Epistle of John* 2.11, quoted in Brown, *Augustine of Hippo*, 325.

20. George Herbert, "The Pulley," in *George Herbert: The Complete Poetry*, eds. John Drury and Victoria Moul (London: Penguin, 2015), 152–53.

21. Augustine, *Confessions*, trans. Henry Chadwick (New York: Oxford University Press, 2008), 3.

22. Dietrich Bonhoeffer to Eberhard Bethge, May 20, 1944, in *Dietrich Bonhoeffer Works*, vol. 8, *Letters and Papers from Prison*, eds. Christian Gremmels et al., trans. Isabel Best et al. (Minneapolis: Fortress, 2010), 394.

23. Bonhoeffer to Bethge, December 18, 1943, in *Letters and Papers from Prison*, 228, emphasis added.

24. Dietrich Bonhoeffer, *Dietrich Bonhoeffer Works*, vol. 6, *Ethics*, eds. Ilse Tödt et al., trans. Reinhard Krauss, Charles C. West, and Douglas W. Stott (Minneapolis: Fortress, 2009), 401.

25. Erich Auerbach, *Mimesis: The Representation of Reality in Western Thought* (Princeton, NJ: Princeton University Press, 2013), 42–43. David Bentley Hart extrapolates: "Nowhere previously in the literature of antiquity had the tears of a rustic been treated as anything but an object of mirth; certainly to regard them as worthy of attention, as grave or meaningful or tragic or expressive of a profound human grief, could appear only grotesque from the vantage of a classical, noble aesthetic." *The Beauty of the Infinite: The Aesthetics of Christian Truth* (Grand Rapids, MI: Eerdmans, 2004), 125.

26. Walker Percy, "Another Message in the Bottle," in *Signposts in a Strange Land*, ed. Patrick Samway (New York: Farrar, Straus and Giroux, 1991), 365–66. "In a very real way, one can say that the Incarnation not only brought salvation to mankind but gave birth to the novel" ("Another Message," 366).

27. Richard Bauckham cites this New Testament tendency to call people by name as an evidence that the Bible is actually intending to be a firsthand account. *Jesus and the Eyewitnesses: The Gospels as Eyewitness Testimony*, 2nd ed. (Grand Rapids, MI: Eerdmans, 2017), 290.

28. Friedrich Nietzsche, *On the Genealogy of Morals*, ed. Walter Kaufmann, trans. Walter Kaufmann and R. J. Hollingdale (New York: Vintage Books, 1989), 144.

29. Romano Guardini, *The Lord* (Washington, DC: Regnery, 1982), 124.

30. Guardini, *The Lord*, 125.

31. *Coco*, directed by Lee Unkrich (Emeryville, CA: Pixar Animation Studios, 2017).

32. Gustavo Gutiérrez, *On Job: God-Talk and the Suffering of the Innocent*, trans. Matthew J. O'Connell (Maryknoll, NY: Orbis Books, 1987), 72.

33. "Strong's G346—Anakephalaioō," Blue Letter Bible, accessed April 22, 2019, www.blueletterbible.org/lang/lexicon/lexicon.cfm?Strongs=G346&t=KJV.

34. "The Word has saved what was created—namely, humanity which had perished. He accomplished this by taking it unto himself and seeking its salvation. The thing which had perished had flesh and blood. The Lord, taking dust from the earth, formed humanity; and it was for humanity that all the dispensation of the Lord's advent took place. He himself therefore had flesh and blood, so that he could recapitulate in himself, not something else, but the original handiwork of the Father, seeking out what had perished. And because of this the apostle, in the Letter to the Colossians, says, 'And you who were once estranged and hostile in mind, doing evil deeds, he has now reconciled in his fleshly body through death, so as to present you holy and blameless and irreproachable before him' [Col. 1:21–22]. He says, 'You have been reconciled in his fleshly body,' because his righteous flesh has reconciled that flesh which was kept in bondage to sin and brought it into friendship with God." James R. Payton Jr., *Irenaeus on the Christian Faith: A Condensation of Against Heresies* (Cambridge: James Clarke, 2012), 166.

35. "The Logos whose excellence is incomparable, ineffable and inconceivable in himself is exalted beyond all creation and even beyond the idea of difference and distinction. This same Logos, whose goodness is revealed and multiplied in all the things that have their origin in him, with the degree of beauty appropriate to each being, *recapitulates all things in himself* (Eph. 1:10)." Maximus, *Ambiguum 7*, in *On the Cosmic Mystery of Jesus Christ: Selected Writings from St Maximus the Confessor*, trans. Paul M. Blowers and Robert Louis Wilken (Crestwood, NY: St. Vladimir's Seminary Press, 2003), 55. Christ is the Logos, the divine Word, through whom all creation has its being and its becoming.

36. Bonhoeffer to Bethge, December 18, 1943, in *Letters and Papers from Prison*, 229–30.

37. C. S. Lewis, "The Weight of Glory," in *"The Weight of Glory" and Other Addresses* (New York: Macmillan, 1949), 15. "You have never talked to a mere mortal. Nations, cultures, arts, civilization—these are mortal, and their life is to ours as the life of a gnat. But it is immortals whom we joke

with, work with, marry, snub, and exploit—immortal horrors or everlasting splendours.… Next to the Blessed Sacrament itself, your neighbour is the holiest object presented to your senses." "The Weight of Glory," 15.

CHAPTER 9

1. Thomas à Kempis, *The Imitation of Christ* (New York: Cosimo, 2007), 43.

2. Taken from the title of Marilyn Vancil's book *Self to Lose, Self to Find* (Enumclaw, WA: Redemption, 2016).

3. Paul Tripp writes, "If you are ever going to be an ambassador in the hands of a God of glorious and powerful grace, you must die. You must die to your plans for your own life. You must die to your self-focused dreams of success. You must die to your demands for comfort and ease. You must die to your individual definition of the good life. You must die to your demands for pleasure, acclaim, prominence, and respect. You must die to your desire to be in control. You must die to your hope for independent righteousness. You must die to your plans for others. You must die to your cravings for a certain lifestyle or that particular location. You must die to your own kingship. You must die to the pursuit of your own glory in order to take up the cause of the glory of Another. You must die to your control over your own time. You must die to your maintenance of your own reputation. You must die to having the final answer and getting your own way. You must die to your unfaltering confidence in you. You must die." Paul David Tripp, *Dangerous Calling* (Wheaton, IL: Crossway, 2012), 189–90.

4. A point Randy Alcorn makes in *Happiness* (Carol Stream, IL: Tyndale, 2015), 335–42.

5. Jonathan Edwards, *The Works of Jonathan Edwards*, vol. 2, *Religious Affections*, ed. John E. Smith (New Haven, CT: Yale University Press, 1959), 257.

6. Edwards, *Religious Affections*.

7. Julia Ward Howe, "The Battle Hymn of the Republic," 1861, public domain.

8. For more on how union with Christ is the anchor and engine of holiness, see Rankin Wilbourne, *Union with Christ: The Way to Know and Enjoy God* (Colorado Springs: David C Cook, 2016), 171–89.

9. J. I. Packer, *A Quest for Godliness: A Puritan Vision of the Christian Life* (Wheaton, IL: Crossway, 1990), 202.

10. Friedrich Nietzsche, *The Complete Works of Friedrich Nietzsche*, vol. 5, *Dawn: Thoughts on the Presumptions of Mortality*, trans. Brittain Smith (Redwood City, CA: Stanford University Press, 2011), 435.

11. Friedrich Nietzsche, *Beyond Good and Evil: Prelude to a Philosophy of the Future*, trans. Helen Zimmern (New York: Macmillan, 1907), 107.

12. Nietzsche, *Dawn*, 435.

13. Annie Dillard, *The Writing Life* (New York: Harper Perennial, 2013), 32.

14. Thérèse, *Story of a Soul: The Autobiography of Saint Thérèse of Lisieux*, ed. Marc Foley, trans. John Clarke (Washington, DC: ICS Publications, 2005), 54. The summary of Thérèse's life is based on James Martin, S. J., *My Life with the Saints* (Chicago: Loyola, 2006), 32–35.

15. Thérèse, *Story of a Soul*, 205.

16. Thérèse, *Story of a Soul*, 244.

17. Thérèse, *Story of a Soul*, 244.

18. Roy Hession and Revel Hession, *The Calvary Road* (Fort Washington, PA: Christian Literature Crusade, 1995), 25.

19. H. Mosser, ed., *The Heidelberg Catechism and the Catechist's Assistant* (Reading, PA: Daniel Miller, 1895), 8.

20. Alongside Thérèse's memoir, one of the most beautiful and challenging summaries of the Christian life was written by John Calvin in what has come to be called "The Golden Book," in which Calvin shows that the sum of the Christian life is the denial of ourselves. He writes: "We are consecrated and dedicated to God in order that we may thereafter think, speak, meditate, and do, nothing except to his glory.... If we, then, are not our own but the Lord's, it is clear what error we must flee, and whither we must direct all the acts of our life. We are not our own: let not our reason nor our will, therefore, sway our plans and deeds.... We are not our own: in so far as we can, let us therefore forget ourselves and all that is ours. Conversely, we are God's: let us therefore live for him and die for him. We are God's: let his wisdom and will therefore rule all our actions.... O, how much has that man profited who, having been taught that he is not his own, has taken away dominion and rule from his own reason that he may

yield it to God! For, as consulting our self-interest is the pestilence that most effectively leads to our destruction, so the sole haven of salvation is to be wise in nothing and to will nothing through ourselves but to follow the leading of the Lord alone." *Calvin: Institutes of the Christian Religion*, ed. John T. McNeill, trans. and indexed Ford Lewis Battles (Philadelphia: The Westminster Press, 1960), 3.7.2, 690. What freedom there must be in laying aside self-concern, in seeing self-interest not simply as a vice but a pestilence, and therefore uprooting vain ambition and relinquishing our thirst for recognition, our desire for distinction. If only we could see and agree that consulting our self-interest is not a privilege of our freedom but a pestilence to our soul, that far from leading to our satisfaction will instead lead to our diminishment, even our destruction.

21. Pierre Hadot, *Philosophy as a Way of Life: Spiritual Exercises from Socrates to Foucault*, ed. Arnold I. Davidson, trans. Michael Chase (Malden, MA: Blackwell Publishing, 1995), 265.

22. See Werner Jaeger's three volume *Paideia*. For any student who wants to understand the classical view of character formation, Jaeger's trilogy is foundational.

23. Hadot, *Philosophy as a Way of Life*.

24. Dallas Willard writes, "Currently we are not only saved by grace; we are paralyzed by it. There is deep confusion. We find it hard to see that grace is not opposed to *effort*, but is opposed to *earning*." *The Great Omission: Reclaiming Jesus's Essential Teachings on Discipleship* (New York: HarperOne, 2014), 166.

25. Matthew Myer Boulton, *Life in God: John Calvin, Practical Formation, and the Future of Protestant Theology* (Grand Rapids, MI: Eerdmans, 2011).

26. Evagrius of Pontus, *Talking Back: A Monastic Handbook for Combating Demons*, trans. David Brakke (Trappist, KY: Cistercian, 2009). For Evagrius, the practice of talking back was often in the context of spiritual warfare.

27. For a short introduction, see appendix 1 to Greg Lukianoff and Jonathan Haidt, *The Coddling of the American Mind: How Good Intentions and Bad Ideas Are Setting Up a Generation for Failure* (New York: Penguin, 2018), 275–78.

28. Benedict, *The Rule of Saint Benedict in English*, ed. Thomas Fry (Collegeville, MN: Liturgical, 1982), 28.

29. Again, this is a staple of CBT. See the classic *Feeling Good* by David Burns. This book is now dated but is a classic on CBT and the notion that feeling follows thinking. The insight is not original to Burns. It's ancient wisdom.

30. See Eugene Peterson, *Eat This Book: A Conversation in the Art of Spiritual Reading* (Grand Rapids, MI: Eerdmans, 2006) for a full-length treatment of this theme.

31. Sarah A. Schnitker, in Anna Goldfarb, "How to Be a More Patient Person," *New York Times*, November 5, 2018, www.nytimes.com/2018/11/05 /smarter-living/how-to-be-a-more-patient-person.html.

32. John Ortberg, *The Life You've Always Wanted: Spiritual Disciplines for Ordinary People*, rev. ed. (Grand Rapids, MI: Zondervan, 2002), 42.

33. Schnitker, in Goldfarb, "How to Be a More Patient Person."

34. Oswald Chambers, *My Utmost for His Highest*, ed. James Reimann, updated ed. (Grand Rapids, MI: Discovery House, 2017), October 21.

CONCLUSION

1. I'm indebted to Dr. Craig Barnes for his reflections on Simon of Cyrene. M. Craig Barnes, "Carrying Jesus' Cross," accessed May 30, 2019, http://nationalpres.org/sites/default/files/sermon_bulletins/2002.03.24 .Barnes.pdf.

2. Thomas Merton, *No Man Is an Island* (Boston: Shambhala, 2005), 132.

NOTHING IS MORE CENTRAL OR MORE BASIC THAN OUR UNION WITH CHRIST...

SO WHY HAVE WE MADE IT OPTIONAL?

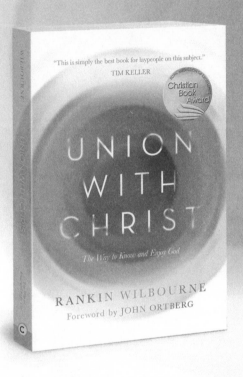

The concept of being one with Jesus is spiritual and mysterious. Yet once it's embraced, nothing is more practical for enjoying the Christian life. Discover how union with Christ is not only possible, but it is possible now. Discover your destiny in Rankin Wilbourne's award-winning book *Union with Christ*.